ORCA **Think**

Question, connect and take action to become better citizens with a brighter future. Now that's smart thinking!

FINDING HOME

The Journey of Immigrants and Refugees

Jen Sookfong Lee

illustrated by Drew Shannon

ORCA BOOK PUBLISHERS

Published in Canada and the United States in 2021 by Orca Book Publishers.
orcabook.com

Library and Archives Canada Cataloguing in Publication
Title: Finding home : the journey of immigrants and refugees /
Jen Sookfong Lee; illustrated by Drew Shannon.
Names: Lee, Jen Sookfong, author. | Shannon, Drew, 1988– illustrator.
Description: Series statement: Orca think | Includes bibliographical references and index.
Identifiers: Canadiana (print) 20200273930 | Canadiana (ebook) 20200273949 |
ISBN 9781459818996 (hardcover) | ISBN 9781459819009 (PDF) | ISBN 9781459819016 (EPUB)
Subjects: LCSH: Human beings—Migration—Juvenile literature. | LCSH: Emigration and immigration—Juvenile literature. | LCSH: Immigrants—Canada—Biography—Juvenile literature.
Classification: LCC GN370 . L44 2021 | DDC j304.8—dc23

Library of Congress Control Number: 2020939258

Summary: A look at how human migration has changed the world. Part of the nonfiction Orca Think series for middle-grade readers, with photographs and illustrations throughout.

Orca Book Publishers is committed to reducing the consumption of nonrenewable resources in the making of our books. We make every effort to use materials that support a sustainable future.

Orca Book Publishers gratefully acknowledges the support for its publishing programs provided by the following agencies: the Government of Canada, the Canada Council for the Arts and the Province of British Columbia through the BC Arts Council and the Book Publishing Tax Credit.

Cover and interior artwork by Drew Shannon
Edited by Sarah N. Harvey
Design by Rachel Page
Author photo by Kyrani Kanavaros

Printed and bound in South Korea.

24 23 22 21 • 1 2 3 4

For my sisters—
daughters of immigrants, generational explorers

Contents

繼往開來

Introduction

I grew up in Vancouver, British Columbia, in a working-class neighborhood on the city's east side, where my friends and their families were from all over the world. There was Shalesh, whose parents had come from Fiji. There was Nadia, whose grandparents had left Italy after World War II. There was Nadine, whose family were members of the Skwxwú7mesh (Squamish) First Nation. There were the Tran brothers, who came from Vietnam after living in a ***refugee camp*** in Hong Kong. And then there was me, Jen. My grandfather arrived in Canada from China in 1913, at the age of 17.

Our diverse neighborhood was the direct result of ***immigration***, which is when people move permanently to a country that is not the one they were born in. By the time I was in elementary school, I knew that everyone's family was different and that their stories—how they came to live in East Vancouver, what they liked to eat, what they believed about religion—were even more diverse. When I visited a friend's house after school, their parents might be cooking stuffed peppers or curried goat or noodle soup, but, just like

Monument for East Vancouver is a sculpture by artist Ken Lum. It marks the route into East Vancouver from the downtown core.
UNSPLASH.COM

my parents, they also supervised homework, tried to get their kids to eat fruits and vegetables, and looked through stacks of bills with worried expressions on their faces. I learned, by watching my friends and their parents, that all of our families were the same at our core. We all wanted to live in a decent house, eat good food and go to good schools, and each parent wanted their children's lives to be happier and safer than their own.

Immigration has always influenced the way in which I observe, learn and make conclusions with an open mind. When you grow up in a diverse community, everyone's home seems different because it's not like your own. In my family's dining room stood a row of porcelain Buddha figures that my mother kept for good luck. The one I remember best sat on an elaborate green chair, holding two peaches in his hands—symbols for a long life. In my friend Lina's house, a portrait of Mary, mother of Jesus, hung above the television, a rosary (a beaded Catholic prayer necklace) draped around the top right-hand corner of the picture. And in Mrs. Fox's house up the street there was a framed hockey jersey on the wall, from her son's career playing in the National Hockey League. These objects came from different cultures, but they were all important to the families I knew. They were symbols of happiness, security and good health.

In this book you'll read about people who leave one country and go to another. Their reasons for leaving may have to do with jobs or school or family. These people are known as ***immigrants***. Sometimes people are forced to move away from their homes because of war, persecution or crime. These people are called ***refugees***. If you live in a country such

Migration Facts

In 2018 Canada welcomed more than 28,000 resettled refugees, the highest number of any country in the world. The United States was second, with just under 23,000, and Australia was third, with 12,700. Significant numbers of resettled refugees were also accepted in the United Kingdom (5,800) and France (5,600).

as Canada, the United States or Australia, all of which have large communities of immigrants and refugees from all over the world, living with people whose cultures are different from yours isn't anything new. Maybe you have friends whose family were immigrants. Maybe you know someone from Syria or the Republic of South Sudan or Guatemala, countries where politics, war and lack of jobs have forced many families to flee their homes and seek safety elsewhere. In chapter 2, you will learn more about how people become immigrants or refugees and what drives them to move to other countries.

A migrant caravan walks into Mexico after crossing the Guatemalan border in 2018.
JOHN MOORE/GETTY IMAGES

You might have heard or read news stories about government policies that are designed to keep people from certain countries from entering others. There are the children from Central America who have been detained (held in custody) in the United States, away from their parents, who are called ***migrants***. The word *migrant* is used for anyone who moves from one country to another but is most commonly used for people who are seeking

A Palestinian child waits his turn to fill water bottles at the al-Shati refugee camp in Gaza City.
KATIB/GETTY IMAGES

asylum or who have been living in poverty and are moving to another country where there are better opportunities for education and work. There are the generations of Palestinian refugees living in the Gaza Strip, a long and narrow area of land that borders Israel on one side and Egypt on another. These refugees, whose numbers are growing in an already densely populated place, are often caught up in the tensions between the State of Palestine, which governs Gaza, and Israel, which controls many aspects of life in Gaza, including trade, water, electricity and border crossings. And there are politicians in other parts of the world who are trying to stop refugees and immigrants from entering their countries altogether, claiming that people who are not born within their borders are threats to security, safety and jobs.

It can be difficult to know, when you read these news stories, whether immigration is a good thing or not. In this book I'll introduce you to people who are or have been immigrants or refugees, whose journeys from their countries of birth to the countries they now call home have been challenging or joyful or long. I'll explain how ***human migration*** can happen and the circumstances that lead to the decision to migrate. And I'll talk about how immigrants shape their communities, what they contribute and how they live. By the end of this book, I hope you can come to your own conclusions about immigrants and refugees. This is a topic that is complicated and sometimes difficult to understand but is also important to our views on the world and the places we live. Because 1 in every 35 people worldwide is a migrant, it's a topic in the news, and one that affects every country, city, neighborhood and school. After all, what would your community look like without human migration? I'm guessing very, very different.

Migration Facts

In 2018, 173,800 children who were unaccompanied by or separated from their families applied for asylum or refugee status. Children under 18 years of age make up 52 percent of the refugee population.

BAHARAK YOUSEFI

How Being a Refugee Child Changed Her Life

In 1988, 13-year-old Baharak Yousefi left Shiraz, Iran, with her parents and flew to Seoul, South Korea. Pretending to be on vacation, they stayed for a month before they paid human smugglers to help them travel to Vancouver, British Columbia, where they made a refugee claim and started their Canadian lives. Their journey across the world, however, had started long before.

In 1978 and 1979, the Iranian Revolution completely changed the country. The Pahlavi dynasty, a *monarchy* (a government with a hereditary leader whose powers can last for life and vary from very few to a dictatorship), was overthrown and replaced by an Islamic republic, which loosely based its laws and policies on a very conservative version of the Islamic religion. Baharak, along with her mother, father and brother, lived through this political upheaval and, later, the strict laws that governed their daily lives. By the time they had decided to leave, the new leader, Ayatollah Khomeini, had implemented laws that restricted the rights of women and girls, as well as free speech. As Baharak explains, "Daily life became more and more difficult and suffocating." It was illegal for her brother to leave the country at all until he had completed his mandatory army service, so Baharak and her parents fled together, and he joined his family three years later.

Baharak as a child before leaving for Canada.
BAHARAK YOUSEFI

Baharak (far left) at school in Shiraz.
BAHARAK YOUSEFI

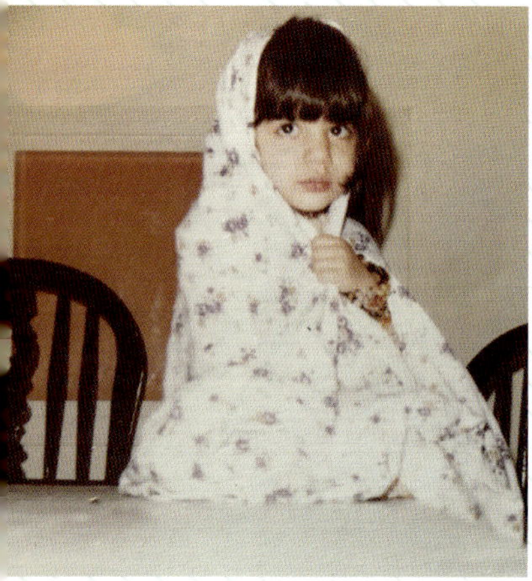

Baharak at home in Shiraz.
BAHARAK YOUSEFI

Like many ***asylum seekers***, Baharak's family made a refugee claim after they had fled to another country instead of fleeing to a refugee camp and going through the ***United Nations Refugee Agency***, which organizes and approves refugee claims worldwide. Baharak and her parents were able to live in Vancouver while their claim was assessed. "My strongest memory of the early days is the swimming pool and TV room at the old YWCA in downtown Vancouver, where we were housed for the first three to four weeks," she recalls. "I could not believe my luck at being able to swim every day and watch *Nightmare on Elm Street* on TV! I was 13 years old, and everything seemed so exciting."

As the Yousefi family settled in, however, challenges started to emerge. Baharak's father, with his limited English, found work as an overnight clerk at a 7-Eleven convenience store. His pay just covered the basics of food, clothing and shelter. Baharak started high school and found it to be a roller coaster of emotions and experiences. "I wasn't able to communicate at all those first few months and only took English as a Second Language [ESL], math and physical education [PE]," she explains. "I loved the ESL classes. The teachers were kind, and I felt like I was in similar company, but math and PE were terrible. I was bullied relentlessly by the 'Canadian' kids, most of the time right in front of the teachers. I hid this from my parents because I felt ashamed and didn't want to add to their already difficult lives."

As time passed, Baharak learned more and more English and started to feel more included, but those stressful years took their toll. "I was depressed a lot and begged my parents to return to Iran," she tells me.

Baharak is now a librarian at Simon Fraser University in Burnaby, British Columbia, where she manages communications. She has always been especially interested in how libraries can help those who are challenged by poverty, culture and other types of ***marginalization***. Her experience as a child refugee is directly related to her focus on inclusion and belonging. "I think adversity has made me a human being who can imagine lives, perspectives and desires different than my own," she says. "It has made me more open—and loving, to be honest—toward other cultures. I guess what I am trying to say is empathy, genuine curiosity and imagination are things you gain when 'you've been there.' Sometimes it feels like that's such a high price to pay."

As an adult now looking back at her childhood, Baharak can see that in most ways, she wasn't so different from the children who picked on her. "The only difference between a refugee and a non-refugee is luck. Luck is the only thing that divides someone like me and someone born in Canada or the United States."

She is right, of course, and children who are refugees want and need the same things we all do: a safe home, access to education and a happy family.

Baharak today, on a trip to learn about other cultures.
BAHARAK YOUSEFI

One
The History of Human Migration

Before there were rules controlling immigration and refugees, humans were already moving around the world. This chapter explores the history of this early migration, the reasons families and communities looked for different places to settle and how this migration changed over time.

THE VERY BEGINNING

Human migration—the movement of people away from their homes to establish new homes in other places—has been occurring throughout history. Humans have been moving across the globe for 70,000 years or longer. Some theories trace our origins to Africa, with groups moving north to the Middle East and then east to Asia and west to Europe, before settling in North, Central and South America. They likely traveled on foot and by boat, some groups staying in their chosen homes while others moved on, motivated by food sources, climate and a sense of adventure. Scientists use the

Migration Facts

The earliest fossil evidence we have of modern humans was found in Ethiopia and is about 200,000 years old.

The ancient Aztecs ruled an empire in what is now Mexico from 1345 to 1521 CE.
JOHN ELK III/GETTY IMAGES

study of DNA and genetics, fossils and cultural storytelling to piece together the history of migration. No one can say for sure how people came to live all over the world, and there are many stories from all cultures that offer different versions of how communities grew. What is certain is that the urge to travel and seek a better life somewhere else is as old as humans themselves.

With humans moving and living all over the world, communities formed, and people began establishing farms, cities, countries and eventually governments. The empires of Egypt, Greece and Rome, the kingdoms of western Europe, Africa and those of the Maya in Mexico and Central America, the dynasties of China, the Blackfoot and Haudenosaunee Confederacies across North America—when people came together, they developed rules for their communities. These rules governed all aspects of life, such as law, money and healthcare. They also began to govern immigration—the movement of people *into* their communities, as well as ***emigration***—the movement of people *out* of their communities.

Migration Facts

There are competing theories about who the earliest North American visitors were. These include Irish monks in the 6th century, Vikings in the 10th century and Chinese explorers in the 15th century.

COLONIZATION AND ITS IMPACT ON MIGRATION

Community rules, also known as policies, evolved over time to suit what was needed, but also to accommodate where the communities were located and where they were moving. Some ancient empires, like the Roman Empire and the Aztec Empire in Mexico, used violence, terror and war to gain control of areas that had things they wanted or needed—people (whom they used for labor) or resources (like gold or spices). This process is called ***colonization***—one group of people forces its way into another people's community and takes control of their government, population and resources. The English and French colonized North America starting at the end of the 15th century. The Dutch colonized Indonesia and South Africa in the 17th century. And Japan colonized Korea in the early 20th century. And these are just a few examples.

British colonial administrator Sir John Arthur Herbert and his wife, Mary, arrive in Calcutta (now Kolkata). He served as governor of Bengal from 1939 until his death in 1943.
KEYSTONE/HULTON ARCHIVE/GETTY IMAGES

Moving On

At its peak the British Empire covered 25 percent of the world's land and included 412 million people. The empire collapsed in large part because of World War II, which was fought in many of its territories and which led to many former colonies transitioning into independent nations in the war's aftermath.

Colonization was, for many years, one of biggest reasons people moved around the world. The British Empire, which flourished from the late 1600s until the mid-20th century, had control of over 60 countries and territories worldwide, including, at different times, Kenya, Trinidad, Jamaica, India, Australia, Singapore and Canada. The empire was so vast that there was a popular saying, "The sun never sets on the British Empire," to describe its geographical reach, which covered the most land area of any empire in history.

Members of the military were usually the first to settle in a colonized country. Once they had established a presence, other people followed. Resources such as lumber and metals, and goods such as spices and fabrics, traveled between colonies and back to the colonizing country. These resources and goods were accompanied by people, some of whom stayed where they had traveled to. These people were, for example, shopkeepers, traders, hunters, farmers and religious leaders. Often their families came with them. As communities grew, they began to include teachers, doctors, nurses and many others needed to help a community survive.

Within a domain such as the British Empire, the movement of people went both ways, with people from the colonies often moving to the colonizing country. The British colonized India and often employed local people in their businesses and homes. If they returned to England, they often brought these employees or servants with them, who would then establish families and lives there.

In addition, people moved between colonies, often going wherever there were job opportunities. For example, in the 19th and 20th centuries, people from India immigrated to Singapore, which was also a British colony, to help with its rapid development. Many were convicts, whose prison sentences were converted to labor in Singapore. Others moved voluntarily, seeing opportunity in what was quickly becoming a fast-paced, Western-style city.

In much of Australia, British convicts were used to provide free labor to a growing country, and they often stayed when their sentences expired. While many of these laborers struggled with adapting to life once they were freed, some of them established businesses and started families. Mary Reibey, once a convicted horse stealer in Britain, rose to prominence as a businesswoman who imported and exported goods and developed real estate. She died in 1855, and in 1994 Australia's government printed her portrait on the country's $20 bill.

Moving On

During the 1850s and 1860s, 30,000 Black slaves fled from the American South to Canada, where ***slavery*** was illegal. They used a secret network of people, homes and transportation called the Underground Railroad. One of the most famous organizers was a former slave named Harriet Tubman, who personally helped bring 300 people over the border. American slave owners put a $40,000 bounty on her head, a huge amount of money for the time.

THE DARK SIDE OF COLONIALISM

Colonialism, while helping the colonizing country grow in geography and riches, had a devastating impact on the regions that were colonized. Often the colonizers used violence and aggression to gain control of the land, people

and resources they wanted. They killed anyone who organized efforts to oppose them, attempted to eradicate the local languages and cultures and forced people to move from their homes to reservations or other segregated areas.

In South Africa, the colonizing Dutch instituted a system of racial segregation, which were rules that forced Black people to live in separate areas and use separate public facilities (swimming pools and schools), barred them from certain professions and areas of study, and limited the amount of contact they could have with white people. This was called apartheid, and it was in effect from 1948 to 1991. It is similar to the "Jim Crow" laws that were enacted in the United States after slavery was repealed in 1865. Those laws sought to keep

A segregated water fountain on the county courthouse lawn in North Carolina in 1938. JOHN VACHA/FPG/GETTY IMAGES

Indigenous children attended residential schools across Canada for more than 100 years. The last residential school closed in 1996.
HULTON ARCHIVE/GETTY IMAGES

the newly freed Black people separated from whites and determined where and how Black people could go to school or work and whom they could marry.

Canada's residential school system, which began in the 1880s and was managed by the government as well as church groups, required that Indigenous children be forcibly removed from their families and placed in schools where they were punished for speaking their first languages and where they were often emotionally, physically and sexually abused. The stated purpose of this was to provide a European-style education and religious training, but it also was intended to erase Indigenous culture and break children's ties with their families. The last residential school closed its doors in 1996, but the effects are still felt by generations of Indigenous people. In 2008 the Truth and Reconciliation Commission of Canada was formed to listen to and gather stories of the residential schools from survivors and witnesses, and to educate people across Canada about the residential school legacy.

Moving On

In 2018 Nadia Murad, who was trafficked from northern Iraq at the age of 19, won the Nobel Peace Prize. In 2016 she became the first ***human-trafficking*** survivor to serve as a United Nations goodwill ambassador. In her role, she educates about the realities of human trafficking and advocates for justice for victims of war crimes everywhere. Nadia was kidnapped with other Yazidi women and girls from northern Iraq by ISIS, an extremist group that has violently fought for control over parts of the Middle East and sought to eliminate the Yazidi people (an act that is called genocide), whom they regard as anti-Muslim. For over a year Nadia was raped and beaten, until she finally escaped and fled as a refugee to Germany.

Two girls pick cotton on a plantation by the Mississippi River in 1950. DOREEN SPOONER/KEYSTONE FEATURES/GETTY IMAGES

Moving On

When Adolf Hitler came to power in Germany in 1933 and began putting laws in place that restricted the education and employment of Germany's Jewish population, many people made plans to leave. Within six years more than 300,000 Jewish people fled to countries around the world, even though some countries refused to offer sanctuary.

In 2015 the commission published a report of its findings. Its documents are now all housed in the National Centre for Truth and Reconciliation at the University of Manitoba.

Colonization is also connected to slavery. European countries such as France, Britain and Portugal kidnapped and transported people from West Africa to work as slaves in Europe, as well as in their colonies in the Caribbean and the Americas, where there was land to farm and not enough people to produce the results at the speed the colonizers wanted. Many slaves eventually ended up in the southern United States, on plantations where cotton, sugar and other crops were grown. These slaves are the ancestors of many of today's Black Americans. From the middle of the 15th century until the mid-19th century, slavery accounted for the forced migration of millions of African people—as many as 25 million. Large numbers of them died during the journey by boat (called the Middle Passage) from West Africa to Europe and from there to the United States. In their new "homes," they worked long hours, their children were often taken away from them and sold, and they endured violent abuse at the hands of their owners, who often treated them like animals. Slavery in the United States ended in 1865 with the end of the Civil War, but policies to maintain racial segregation were not struck down until the Civil Rights Act was passed in 1964.

Slavery still exists in some parts of the world in different forms. Human trafficking is a multibillion-dollar business and one of the fastest-growing illegal industries on the planet. People who live in countries where there is little opportunity for work and education are the most vulnerable to human trafficking, because they are often desperate to believe the promises they are given. For example, they may be promised a new life in a wealthy country such as the United States, with a well-paying job and free travel to their destination.

Sometimes when a country is at war, people are captured and trafficked, mostly women and girls, and usually for sex work. Statistics in a 2019 report by the United Nations show that 30 percent of human-trafficking victims are children, with the majority from sub-Saharan Africa and East Asia.

At-risk people are forced to work illegally, with no one monitoring how many hours they work or what their working conditions are like. Some may work as servants in private homes. Women (and some men) may be forced to work in brothels, which are businesses where customers pay for sex. If someone has been forced into slavery, they are given no money for the work they do—all of their "earnings" go to pay the organization that has enslaved them. And because they have been forced into unpaid work in a country where their presence is ***undocumented***, they are unable to reach out to local authorities for help.

Sometimes workers from other countries are called ***indentured laborers***, which means they have been promised payment and/or freedom once they have worked for

Migration Facts

In the 19th century and early part of the 20th century, the United States received waves of poor immigrants from Europe, including 4.5 million from Ireland and 5 million from Germany, who were seeking prosperity in a new country.

a certain amount of time to pay off their debt to the traffickers. The difference between slavery and indentured labor is slight, especially given that the debt these workers believe they are paying off can keep growing if the organization provides shelter or food. With an ever-growing debt and years of working to pay it off, indentured laborers can work in difficult conditions for the bulk of their lives, in a country they never have an opportunity to explore or understand. After all, if these laborers are working in a sweatshop or family home all day long, with time off only to sleep, they have very little opportunity to become integrated into their surroundings.

Moving On

In 1939 a ship called the *St. Louis* arrived off the coast of Florida, carrying 908 Jews fleeing the Holocaust in Germany. The United States refused entry to the passengers, and they were forced to return to Europe, where some were accepted as refugees in Great Britain, France, the Netherlands and Belgium, while others were forced back to Germany. However, 254 of those passengers are known to have died in the Holocaust.

EARLY IMMIGRATION POLICIES

As countries and their borders became more established, and after slavery was abolished in the United States and elsewhere, governments needed to create rules to govern immigration. Countries like Canada needed people to help work in the lumber, mining, fur trade and other resource-based industries to keep up with the demand from Europe, where many of their goods were being sold. The governments who needed labor began to recruit in other countries, depending on the kind of people they wanted. And they needed rules to admit some people while keeping others out.

These policies began to be implemented in the 18th century in Canada, the United States and Australia, countries where there was lots of space and much work to be done, but not enough people to do it. At first Canada promised land and employment to immigrants from Great Britain, and advertised this in articles and newspapers, as well as through immigration agents, who met with people in England.

Starting in the late 1800s and until 1930, the Canadian government, in cooperation with charities in England, brought more than 100,000 children who were orphaned or living in poverty in English cities to Canada, where they worked in homes and on farms. Ranging from 6 to 15 years of age, they were called British Home Children, and they were a source of cheap or free labor as Canada established its farms and cities. Sometimes children were adopted by the families they lived with. But mostly they were seen as hired help, which meant they worked long, grueling hours and were often mistreated by their employers. When they reached adulthood (age 16), they could do as they wanted and live where they pleased, but they often had had no education or training beyond what they'd learned in their Canadian homes.

In the early days of settlement in Canada, immigrants also came from other countries, including China, Japan and India, but these people were not promised land, and their jobs, which were often dangerous, were only temporary.

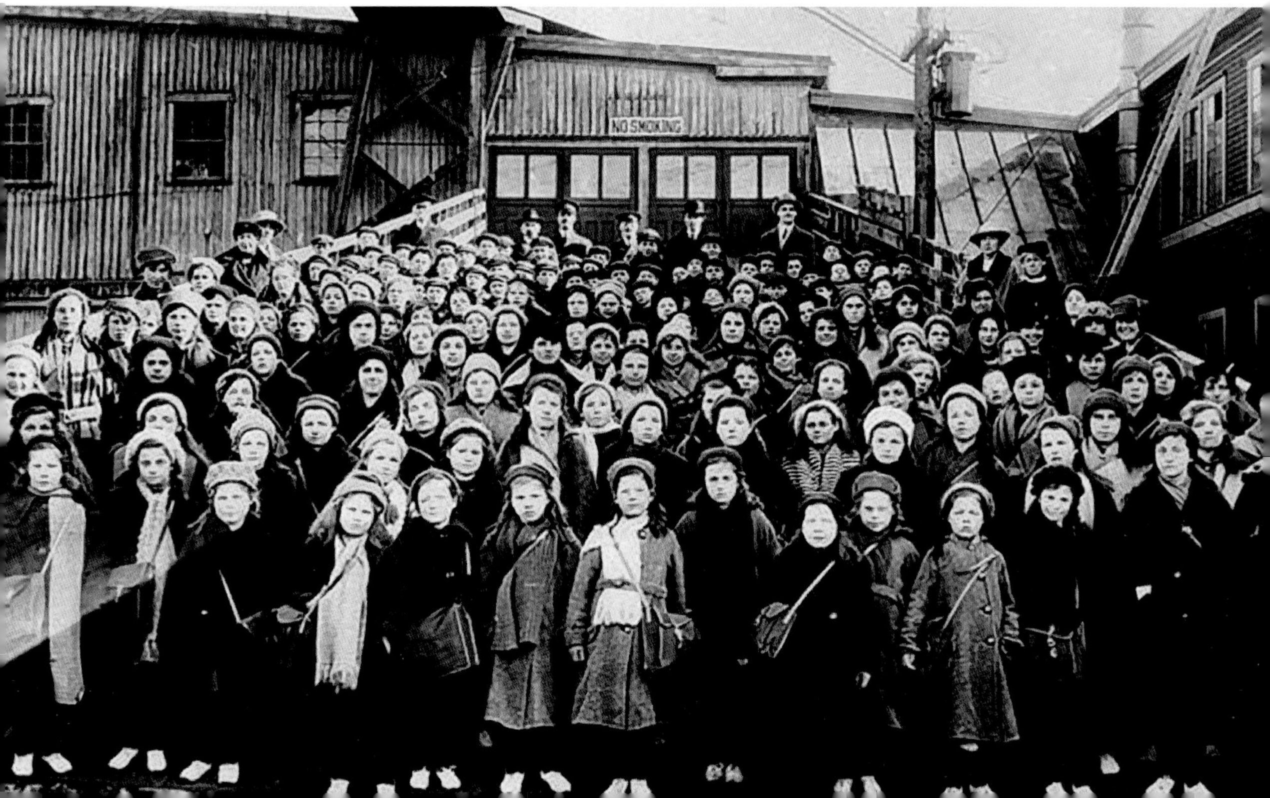

A group of British Home Children arrives in Saint John, NB. LIBRARY AND ARCHIVES CANADA/ DEPARTMENT OF THE INTERIOR FONDS/A041785

There were 340 Sikhs, 24 Muslims and 12 Hindus on the *Komagata Maru*. The ship was moored in Vancouver Harbour for two months before being forced to sail back to India in July 1914. LEONARD FRANK, 1914, VANCOUVER PUBLIC LIBRARY, ACCESSION # 6232

For example, a company hired by the Government of Canada recruited over 17,000 Chinese men to build the railway system across the western province of British Columbia. These men were paid one dollar a day, while white workers were paid twice that and sometimes even more. The Chinese workers were given the riskiest jobs, such as placing explosives in mountainsides for tunnels, and they often died as a result. When the railway was completed, many workers who had survived lived the rest of their lives in poverty, separated from their families, never having made enough money to pay for a passage back to China.

Immigration policy was based on labor needs, but it also reflected racial biases. Groups from western and northern Europe were accepted with the most ease, while people from southern and eastern Europe were not considered as favourably. People from East Asia and South Asia received the worst treatment of all. In 1914 passengers on a ship called the *Komagata Maru* were not allowed to disembark in Vancouver because the government did not want the 350 people from India to settle in Canada. The ship remained in the harbor for two months, with limited water and food, until it was forced to sail back to India. There it was met by British soldiers who killed 20 of the passengers during the subsequent riot. In 2016 Prime Minister Justin Trudeau made a formal apology for Canada's role, speaking in the House of Commons and directly to some descendants of the passengers on the *Komagata Maru*.

Immigration policy that excluded groups based on race was in place in Australia and the United States as well. The Immigration Restriction Act, established in Australia in 1901, was designed to keep out immigrants who were not white, and it stated that all people who wished to settle in Australia had to pass a language test in a European language. People of color were thought to be dirty and criminal-minded, an idea that made little sense, especially in Australia, which until 1868, only 33 years earlier, had been partially settled by white British convicts.

In the United States, the Immigration Act of 1924 worked on a quota system. People from some countries, such as Japan, were not allowed to settle at all, and people from others, such as eastern and southern europe, were allowed in on a limited basis. The goal was to keep the population as western and northern european—in other words, white—as possible, with the exception of slaves or temporary workers. Immigration to the United States opened up after 1965, with people coming from Africa, Asia and Latin America. Currently, however, immigration policy is changing yet again, as the United States government has made moves to restrict immigrants from Africa, the Middle East and Latin America.

A mother and her two daughters walk to a port of entry at the Mexico–United States border to ask for asylum.
MARIO TAMA/GETTY IMAGES

Three boys at the Pelican Lake Indian Residential School in Ontario. Indigenous children were typically forced to leave their families and attend residential school when they were six years old, sometimes younger.
ARCHIVES OF ONTARIO
C330 13-0-0-162

WHAT IS DECOLONIZATION?

You may have heard the word ***decolonization*** in the news or at school. Historically, the term is used when a government hands over control to one of its colonies, allowing the colony to achieve governmental and financial independence. For example, the Philippines was once a colony of Spain, until the country was purchased by the United States in 1902. During World War II the Philippines was occupied by the Japanese, and afterward, in 1946, the United States granted the Philippines its independence.

But decolonization can also mean the long process of acting to undo some of the harm that a government or system has caused to people who have historically been discriminated against. For example, in North America today there is a strong movement by Indigenous Peoples to decolonize, which means that different Indigenous groups and individuals are in the process of strengthening their ties to their traditional cultures, languages and traditions. When the governments of Canada and the United States removed Indigenous Peoples from their traditional lands and forced children to enter residential schools, these communities lost their languages and their ways of life. As decolonization progresses, they are relearning languages, rituals and home building, hunting and other traditional skills that have been suppressed for generations.

Throughout the history of human migration and even today, people have voluntarily left their homes in search of a better life. Sometimes that is because they want access to more money or resources. Sometimes it's because their homes and lives are threatened by war or violence. But the basic reason is the same: they believe that moving somewhere else will help them be happier.

In the next chapter, we will discuss refugees and how conditions in their home communities push them to move all over the world. But first, let's hear stories from three families who left their home country by choice to seek a better life.

Migration Facts

Some countries that were once colonies are Bermuda, Greenland, Costa Rica, Kenya, Jamaica, Haiti and Peru.

Migrants wait in line at the Mexico–United States border in 2019.
MARIO TAMA/GETTY IMAGES

GABY, JUAN AND MAYA GOMEZ

A Traveling Family

In 2002 Gaby and Juan Gomez arrived in Vancouver, Canada, from Guadalajara, Mexico, as skilled immigrants. Both Gaby and Juan were industrial engineers, and they came to Canada with the intention of experiencing a different country and culture and embark on an adventure.

Gaby and Juan Gomez decided to make a new life for their family in Canada.
GABY GOMEZ

"We had started a small clothing factory that had to close at one point," Gaby explains. "We had to begin again looking for jobs and a new place to live, and we decided it would be no different to do it in a different country. It also added an adventure to our lives!"

Canada seemed like a natural fit. "Juan had lived and worked in Vancouver after high school and loved the city ever since. It is also close to Mexico and Guadalajara, with much better weather than other parts of Canada. Still, some people in Mexico ask us if there are igloos here," Gaby tells me, laughing.

Soon after arriving, Gaby found a temporary job working at Subway. "I was a sandwich artisan," she says. Juan sold lottery tickets. After several months of support from a job-finding club that helps recent immigrants, both Gaby and Juan found work as engineers. In 2006 their daughter, Maya, was born. The family now also includes Marieto, a rescue cat.

As immigrant parents, Gaby and Juan aim to make sure their Mexican roots are always alive in their home. "It starts with speaking only Spanish at home and exposing Maya to movies, television and books in Spanish," they tell me. "We also found a school whose second language is Spanish and where she has several opportunities to show and tell about Mexico."

Like many families, the Gomezes use celebrations as a learning experience. "Holidays are another big opportunity to bring our culture back to life, from the Day of the Dead to Nativity at Christmas to the Coming of the Wise Men to using piñatas during her birthday parties." Making sure Maya is connected to the culture of Mexico involves daily conversation. "We are constantly using our experiences living in Mexico and how different it is to life in Canada as teaching tools. Every time we visit Mexico, we highlight this for her."

In fact, Maya is fascinated by how customs differ from place to place. "She loves the differences, especially not having an early bedtime while there," Gaby says. "She also finds 'breaking rules' funny and intriguing, like how it is common in Mexico to cross in the middle of the street or not wear a helmet while riding a bike."

The breaking of a piñata is a Mexican cultural tradition that has gained popularity all over the world.
DES/GETTY IMAGES

What I find so fascinating about Gaby, Juan and Maya is how they make learning about culture—all cultures—a family experience. In 2016 they quit their jobs, packed up their things and traveled around the world for 14 months. "Aside from deciding to move to Canada, [that was] the best decision and experience ever," Gaby tells me. "We learned so much, like how to be detached from owning things and how little we need to be happy and fulfilled. We learned by doing and experiencing, and saw the abysmal differences in livelihoods around the globe. Most people are so happy and generous when one shows interest and respect for their cultures and languages."

The Gomezes' cats, Marieto and Luna. Luna has since passed away.
GABY GOMEZ

When I ask how Maya settled back into home and school in Vancouver after this epic trip, Gaby says, "She missed not having 'time just to be.' Here at home we *have to do this, have to be here*. She learned the value of using time to do and experience what matters most."

Maya, unlike her parents, was born in Canada, and I ask Gaby what she and Juan hope their daughter takes away from her childhood, which is so different from her parents' younger lives. "Sometimes we wish she was more closely exposed to not having so much," Gaby replies. "Like so many people in Mexico and other developing countries, or like us growing up and closely relating to people who struggled for the basic comforts in life. But on the other hand, she is growing up without similar constraints and assumptions of how things are or how they can't be. And so we hope she sees no boundaries in accomplishing whatever she wants."

MISHAL SAEED AND ASIA CAPRI

A Mentor and Immigrant Youth Working Together

Mishal Saeed is a youth worker with a nonprofit organization called MOSAIC, which helps immigrants and refugees in Vancouver, British Columbia, settle into their new lives. In addition to helping young people learn English, find jobs and access counseling, Mishal has also led MOSAIC's popular NuYu (Newcomer Youth) program, which uses theater as a tool to help diverse youth express their emotions, experiences and challenges. "Many youth may hesitate to join a theater program because they may feel shy and may have the fear of being judged," she explains. "But in the NuYu program, the youth begin to open up to one another after playing icebreaker games and being assured that they are in a safe place."

Mishal's interest in her work comes from a personal place. "I was drawn to working with immigrant youth as I can relate to some of their struggles as [part of] a visible minority and being the daughter of immigrants," she tells me. "Being a youth already has its challenges, but when you are in the process of settling into a new country, these challenges can be intensified. Their resilience constantly inspires me, and I always learn from them," she adds.

The benefits run both ways, and theater and performance are effective tools for youth who may feel out of place or isolated. "Participating in theater can benefit youth newcomers as it provides a safe space for them to express themselves," Mishal explains. "Youth are able to get out of their comfort zones by acting and taking on different ideas and characters. Young newcomers are also able to make friends by participating in theater, as the enjoyable environment allows the ice to be broken easily. The feedback we receive from the youth about the program is incredible! The youth agree that the program helps to improve their communication skills and how they deal with discrimination."

Immigrant youth participate in a NuYu theater workshop in Vancouver, BC.
MISHAL SAEED

I ask Asia Capri, a 14-year-old newcomer from Italy, about her experience participating in NuYu. "My favorite thing about NuYu was creating the scenes we would perform and practicing them to make them better," she tells me. Asia had the full support of her mother, who wanted her daughter to make friends and learn new skills. "My mom thought it was a good thing to get out of my comfort zone and be onstage."

At the end of every year, the NuYu participants perform for their friends and family, and the energy is always electric. "It's full of positivity! The youth are often very excited to perform and present the scenes they created, which may be inspired by experiences they had," Mishal says. In fact, many of the youth seem to catch the performing bug. "After the performance, the youth celebrate with their peers and they also ask if they can perform in front of others again!"

As an experienced youth worker, Mishal knows how displaced and disoriented immigrant and refugee children can feel, and she has this piece of advice for all children: "I think it is important for young children to know that living as an immigrant in Canada may have its challenges, so it is important to be mindful of that. I would encourage young children to say hello and to be welcoming to a new classmate who just arrived in Canada, and to offer a helping hand."

DANIEL SAIYO

A Son Reunited with His Mother

In 2001, when Daniel Saiyo was a year old, his mother, Maryann, left him in the care of his grandparents in the Antique province of the Philippines and moved to Canada through the Live-In Caregiver program, which allowed families to hire individuals, mostly women, to care for children, elderly relatives or people with disabilities. Like many women from countries with limited job options, Maryann made the difficult decision to leave her family and start a new life in Canada, where she could earn more money and where there were far more educational and career opportunities for her son. After two years working in eldercare, Maryann applied to become a permanent resident. Then, when she was able, she sponsored her son, by that time seven years old, and he joined her in Vancouver, British Columbia.

As Daniel recalls, his early childhood spent on his grandparents' farm was full of family and community. "Houses were hand built by the residents, along with the help of other neighbors," he explains. "Considering how small my hometown is, everyone knew each other quite well. We would host parties for the entire community. My childhood in the Philippines was spent around my grandparents, aunts and uncles. They did their best to raise me, and I got to know them as my parents and role models." He was happy with his life the way it was, but he also felt the absence of his mother. "Being apart from my mom for six years was a very long time," he says. "I would get occasional phone calls, but that was not enough to keep us close. In those six years I viewed my grandparents as my mother and father." Even now, 12 years later, that separation affects Daniel's life. "My relationship with my mother is not as strong as it might have been but, at the same time it is enough."

Daniel and his mother, Maryann.
DANIEL SAIYO

When it was time for Daniel to leave Antique, he says he felt "heartbroken." As he and Maryann prepared for their flight, they spent a week saying goodbye to friends and family. "After spending so much time with my other relatives, I was attached and did not want to leave," he tells me. Daniel was sad about leaving, but he was also excited by all the experiences the journey included. "It was my first time being on a boat and plane. I was shocked finding out the flight to Canada was extremely long!" Like many newcomers, Daniel was surprised by the winter. "Upon arriving to Canada, the first thing I saw was snow. I was confused, not knowing what it was."

At only seven years old, Daniel transitioned into the Canadian school system without too much trouble. As he explains, "Adapting to life in Canada at a young age is much easier as opposed to when you are older. During the first few days of school I was very quiet, shy and just trying to absorb everything new. As time went by, I was slowly fitting in with the other children and got accustomed to how things are done in Canada." His mother had already built up a strong community to welcome them—friends, relatives and fellow church members. There were plenty of people who spoke Tagalog, a Philippine language (there are over 100,000 people of Philippine descent living in Metro Vancouver) and could help Daniel and Maryann settle into their life as a two-person family. This tight-knit community has helped Daniel figure out his identity. "Being an immigrant, there is one thing I learned, and that is to never forget where you come from."

Every few years Daniel and Maryann visit the Philippines, traveling back to the family farm where Daniel spent his first few years as a young child. Now 19 years old and a proud high-school graduate, he still values his time with his grandparents and other relatives. "My favorite thing to do in the Philippines is to lie down in a hammock outside of the house in the presence of everyone I've been apart from for a very long time," he says. "I also love going for walks up in the mountains where we grow coconuts. A group of us just talk, and when we get hungry or thirsty, one person climbs a tree and tosses some coconuts down."

I think it's safe to say that Daniel will never forget where he came from.

Daniel left the Philippines to join his mom in Canada when he was seven years old, but he and she go back to visit family there every couple of years. MLENNY/GETTY IMAGES

Two

Migration Today

There are many factors that lead people to decide to leave their homes and move elsewhere permanently. Some *push* them to leave, such as war, poverty, political persecution or a lack of educational or work opportunities. Others *pull* them to leave, such as a desirable climate, more jobs, better schools, political stability or family members already established elsewhere.

WHAT MAKES PEOPLE EMIGRATE?

Almost all people who leave their homes consider a combination of ***push and pull factors***, making their decisions based on what they are leaving behind and what they might gain in their new home. Sometimes the decision is more about the *pull*, meaning a person is making the decision on the basis of where they want to be, the place that will best help them achieve their work, schooling or personal goals. This person might want to study a topic that is offered only in universities that are far away. That person might be moving to join their

Moving On

In 2018 there were 68.5 million ***internally displaced persons***, asylum seekers and refugees worldwide, the highest number since the end of World War II. There were:

- 40 million internally displaced people
- 25.4 million refugees
- 3.1 million asylum seekers

These Syrian children live at a Turkish refugee camp. Camps like this can be the size of small cities, housing hundreds of thousands of people.
ORLOK /SHUTTERSTOCK.COM

children in another country. Someone else might be moving because they have been offered a good job in a bigger city.

Sometimes the decision is more about the *push*—their home becomes unlivable due to violence and war or religious and political persecution, and people must flee in order to keep themselves and their families safe. Such persons are called ***forcibly displaced people***. If they stay within their country, perhaps escaping harm by hiding within a city or in the countryside, they are called internally displaced persons. Sometimes people decide they need to leave their country entirely, and they seek international protection. If they have not yet been evaluated by another country or organization that will offer them protection, they are called asylum seekers, because they are still looking for somewhere to go.

Internally displaced persons and asylum seekers become refugees after their claims for protection are evaluated at a refugee camp, by an organization that helps refugees or by the government of a country that they are subsequently

Migration Facts

The five countries that receive the most asylum seekers are Turkey, Pakistan, Uganda, Sudan and Germany. The five countries that resettle the most refugees are Canada, the United States, Australia, the United Kingdom and France.

allowed to live in. They are then helped to build lives in their new country.

Others compelled to seek asylum are ***stateless persons***, people who are not citizens of any country. This can occur if the laws of a country change, which can happen during war, or if the people belong to a group that is being discriminated against and their citizenship is taken away. Without citizenship, a person is not protected by law and cannot access services, obtain employment or attend school.

The terms *immigrant* and *refugee* are quite different. Immigrants have the ability to choose when they leave their homes and under what conditions. My grandfather, who wanted a new home with better job opportunities for himself and his children, chose to move from China to Canada. Even though he wasn't happy with the way people lived in his home village, his move to Canada was entirely his choice. In contrast, a family from Syria, a country embroiled in a violent and years-long civil war, will be forced to become refugees and find asylum elsewhere when their home, neighborhood and city are destroyed by bombs, and civilians—people who are not soldiers, police officers, aid workers or journalists—are dying as a result of this violence.

LEGAL VERSUS ILLEGAL MIGRATION

You've probably heard stories on the news about ***illegal migrants***, people who cross a border and enter a country by violating the immigration rules of that country. This definition may seem simple, but it's actually quite complicated.

Asylum seekers often go to refugee camps first, in areas that are removed from their homes and are relatively safe. But these camps are not where they eventually settle. Since August 2017, Rohingya asylum seekers, who are mostly

Moving On

The largest refugee camps in the world include:

- Kutupalong, in Bangladesh—886,778 people (about the same as the population of San Jose, California)
- Kakuma, in Kenya—184,550 people (about the same size as Knoxville, Tennessee)
- Zaatari, in Jordan—77,781 people (about the same population as Saint-Laurent, Quebec)
- Yida, in South Sudan—70,331 people (similar to Lethbridge, Alberta)
- Panian, in Pakistan—62,264 people (roughly the same size as Rockhampton, Queensland)

A young boy waits for prayer at a Rohingya refugee camp in Bangladesh.
ALLISON JOYCE/GETTY IMAGES

Muslim, have fled religious persecution in Myanmar and escaped to camps in neighboring Bangladesh. Once there, their refugee claims are evaluated by the United Nations Refugee Agency or other government or service agencies. At that point they wait to be accepted in other countries around the world, such as Canada or Australia.

However, not all asylum seekers have the same journey. Some bypass refugee camps altogether and arrive at another country's border unannounced and then file a claim for refugee status. In 2009 two boats from Sri Lanka arrived off the coast of British Columbia, and all 568 Tamil passengers, who were escaping persecution in Sri Lanka, claimed refugee status. Their claims were evaluated in Vancouver, and 230 were accepted. These asylum seekers arrived with little documentation and may have paid smugglers (who work for criminal organizations) to help them travel illegally to other countries.

While aspects of their journey might have been illegal, it is not illegal to seek asylum to escape persecution in your country of origin. Some migrants enter a country illegally, either crossing a border where there are no officials to spot them or by traveling to a country as a visitor or tourist and simply staying past the allowed time. These people may live without documentation for many years.

When Chinese immigration to Canada was severely restricted during the early 20th century, some people arrived with falsified documents or overstayed their visitor visas. In 1947 these restrictions were lifted, and in 1960 the government declared an amnesty (an official pardon) for all illegal Chinese Canadians, allowing them to come forward and apply for citizenship.

Currently the United States is proposing to build a wall on the border it shares with Mexico, which stretches more than 2,000 miles (3,218 kilometers), in order to deter asylum seekers from such countries as Guatemala, Honduras and

Migration Facts

Every year migrants travel 1.24 billion miles (2 billion kilometers) in the process of seeking asylum.

Migration Facts

Each day 44,400 people are forced to flee their homes because of war, violence, famine and persecution.

A migrant caravan grew into the thousands as it moved from Central America to the Mexico–United States border in 2018.
JOHN MOORE/GETTY IMAGES

El Salvador. Because these seekers have not yet been assessed by a refugee agency, some people have called them illegal migrants and are concerned about security at American borders and throughout the country.

So the term *illegal migrant* is complicated. People seeking asylum without refugee documentation may well have committed crimes in their home country, but this doesn't mean their refugee claims are false. For example, Michel Chikwanine, co-author of *Child Soldier: When Boys and Girls Are Used in War*, was kidnapped at age five and forced to be a ***child soldier*** for rebel fighters in the Democratic Republic of Congo before coming to Canada as a refugee at the age of 11. He had committed acts of violence and in Congo would be considered a criminal. However, his refugee claim was accepted because he had been kidnapped as a young child and was forced to take sides in a country torn apart by violence.

Whenever you hear politicians using the term *illegal migrant* to try to sway public opinion, it is important to remember that everyone has a right to seek a safe place to live without fearing violence or persecution because of their race, gender, sexuality, religion or political beliefs. Seeking asylum is not illegal, and when families or individuals come to another country and make a refugee claim, only an agency in charge of approving those claims can decide whether people are allowed to settle in their destination country as refugees or not.

Moving On

In 2013 Southern New Hampshire University started a distance learning program for refugees living in camps, starting with displaced persons in Rwanda. Since then the free education program, backed by charitable donations, has expanded into Kenya, Malawi, South Africa and Lebanon.

IMMIGRATION AND DIVERSITY

Immigration from different parts of the world creates multicultural—or diverse—countries. This means that in any given city in such countries as Canada, Great Britain and the United States, which have long histories of receiving immigrants from all over the world, there are different and dynamic

Three young girls at a Chinese New Year parade in Vancouver, BC. SERGEI BACHLAKOV/ SHUTTERSTOCK.COM

communities of people. In Canada, projections based on current immigration numbers suggest that by 2031, 47 percent of children born to immigrants will belong to a visible minority—that is, people who are not of European descent.

One of the ways diversity is most apparent is in cultural celebrations. Where I live, in Vancouver, British Columbia, there is the Chinese New Year parade, which snakes its way through Chinatown at the end of every winter. There is also the Vaisakhi parade, a celebration that honors the harvest and serves as a joyful event for the large Sikh community. There is even the Hapa-palooza Festival, which celebrates communities of people who are of mixed race, like my son, who has Chinese, Scottish, Irish, Cree and Ukrainian origins. In a diverse city, there is always a holiday to celebrate with food and music!

Multicultural cities often have neighborhoods of people with the same origins, who live together and establish

Members of the Sikh community in Walsall, England, sweep the parade route during Vaisakhi. CHRISTOPHER FURLONG/GETTY IMAGES

businesses and restaurants that remind them of their home countries. This helps them establish their families in their new homes. In Los Angeles there is Koreatown, home to the country's largest concentration of Korean Americans. Established in the 1970s, when many families left South Korea in the aftermath of the Korean War, Koreatown is a dynamic, busy neighborhood famous for its 24-hour businesses, nightclubs, spas and restaurants serving food that is Korean but is also influenced by other immigrant groups from Latin America and South Asia. It's a neighborhood that truly combines elements from all the many different people who live, shop and work there.

These neighborhoods can be old and well established, like Little Italy in New York City, which began growing in the mid-1800s, or they can be younger, started by recent

Italian immigrants began settling in New York City's Little Italy in the late 1800s.
LITTLENYSTOCK/SHUTTERSTOCK.COM

newcomers or by families who moved to other neighborhoods as their jobs and finances changed. For example, although Vancouver's Chinatown is the oldest Chinese neighborhood in the area, with buildings that are over 100 years old, many Chinese families settled in Richmond, a suburb 9 miles (15 kilometers) south of downtown Vancouver, in the 1990s and 2000s. It is in Richmond that the trendiest Chinese supermarkets and restaurants are located and where many Chinese Canadian families decide to raise their children, away from the bustle of the city center.

Diversity can sometimes be difficult for people to understand, especially when immigration is new to that country or when large numbers of people from one particular country arrive over a short period of time. To some people, immigrants represent unwelcome change. Newcomers bring with them different foods, languages and customs, which may seem strange or scary. The fear of a country's personality changing because of immigration can sometimes result in acts of racism, such as the 2019 shootings at two mosques (places of worship for the Islam religion) in Christchurch, New Zealand. Fifty-one people, almost all Muslim, died.

What is important to remember, however, is that without immigration, and the contributions that people from around the world have made, our cities and neighborhoods would not be what they are today. Everything from the food we eat to what we learn in school to the holidays we celebrate would be very, very different without immigrants. And not nearly as interesting!

New Zealand prime minister Jacinda Ardern speaks to members of the Muslim community at al-Noor mosque. It was one of the sites of a tragic shooting in March 2019.
KAI SCHWOERER/GETTY IMAGES

The Richmond Night Market is a Chinese Canadian summertime tradition in Richmond, BC.
SEN YANG/SHUTTERSTOCK.COM

THE JARIDI FAMILY

From Syria to Jordan to Vancouver

Many Syrian families, like the Jaridis, ended up living in tents like these after they fled their homes during the country's civil war.
LIOR MIZRAHI/GETTY IMAGES

In the spring of 2011, peaceful protests broke out in a number of countries in the Middle East, resulting in the resignation of dictators in Tunisia and Egypt. This was called the Arab Spring and was celebrated for how peacefully citizens took their concerns public and triggered democratic change. In Syria, however, a different sequence of events unfolded.

Syria's president, Bashar al-Assad, began to shut down the protests, which were led by a number of different groups, and his military started to violently attack protesters and other citizens. Rebel forces, with backing from other countries, fought back, leading to a civil war that has destroyed much of the country and displaced half of Syria's 22 million people from their homes. Since then 5.6 million refugees have fled, including the Jaridi family, whom I met in Vancouver.

Ibrahim Jaridi was a farmer in the southern city of Daraa, where his family has farmed for generations. In 2012, the year the conflict came to their community, he was living with his wife, Reem Shehadat, a stay-at-home mother, and their two sons, Khaleel and Mohammad, who were four and two. After the war destroyed their house and farmland, the family fled to a refugee camp in Jordan, where they lived for four years, waiting to see when and if they would be granted asylum

in another country. Khaleel, who is now 10, remembers the camp having strict rules. “There was security everywhere, and they didn’t let you get out,” he told me. Everyday activities like school and outdoor play were a challenge. “I had some friends,” Khaleel recalls. “I had to go to the kindergarten place, but it wasn’t really good because there were some homeless people who wanted to eat, and whenever they saw people coming out, they would always say, ‘Give us your food.’ ”

The Zaatari refugee camp in Jordan houses more Syrian refugees than any other camp in the world. In 2020 more than 75,000 people lived there.
EHAB OTHMAN/SHUTTERSTOCK.COM

Even in the camp, however, life went on, and the boys adopted the stray cats who followed them around. Khaleel, remembering the good things about the camp, says, “I touched a cat and it started to be a pet. He used to come to the camp at night. If he didn’t come, it made me a little sad.”

Mohammad, shaking his head, adds, “We forgot to bring our cats to Canada,” a statement that makes his parents laugh.

Eventually the Jaridis’ refugee claim was accepted by the Canadian government, and the family arrived in Vancouver in 2016. The journey was a highlight for the two boys.

"I really liked the bus [from their camp to the airport]. It was humongous. It was a humongo-saurus," Khaleel tells me, his eyes bright with the memory. The family settled in East Vancouver, and Ibrahim got a job at a company that makes equipment for outdoor sports. Reem, in addition to looking after the two boys, takes English classes and volunteers with a support group for Syrian women. Khaleel is in fourth grade and Mohammad is in second, and both have great dreams for the future. "I want to be the principal of Canada, like Justin Trudeau!" Khaleel exclaims.

Mohammad, after thinking for a moment, says, "I want to be John Cena. He fought a bear. A ghost bear."

At the end of our conversation, I ask the boys what they like most about living in Canada. Khaleel mentions the science center, the aquarium and the iPads. Mohammad nods along, but then says quietly, "My favorite thing in Canada is my family." I glance at Reem, who has let her sons do most of the talking, and she reaches out, placing her hand on Mohammad's head, and blinks back tears.

NHUNG N. TRAN-DAVIES

From Child Refugee to Doctor and Author

Nhung N. Tran-Davies is a doctor, social justice advocate and children's author who lives in Alberta. She and her family left Vietnam as refugees in 1978, when Nhung was only five years old. They traveled first by boat across the South China Sea and then spent eight months in a refugee camp in Malaysia. Eventually the family, which included Nhung's single mother and five older siblings, flew to Edmonton. They were welcomed at the airport by a group of Canadians who had helped organize their arrival.

"What I remember most was when we came through the gates of the international airport and we were greeted with love and warmth from a group of Canadians," Nhung recalls. "I especially remember a young girl by the name of Adrienne who came up to me and presented me with a doll. I was overwhelmed with joy. That moment came to define the rest of my life as it represented all the kindness, generosity and compassion of so many Canadians."

Nhung was born in 1973, during the final years of the Vietnam War. Then, Vietnam was very politically unstable and wracked with poverty. Nhung's mother, a widow, did her best to feed and house her six children. "Because of the destruction from the war and hardship and oppression from the communist government that took over our country,

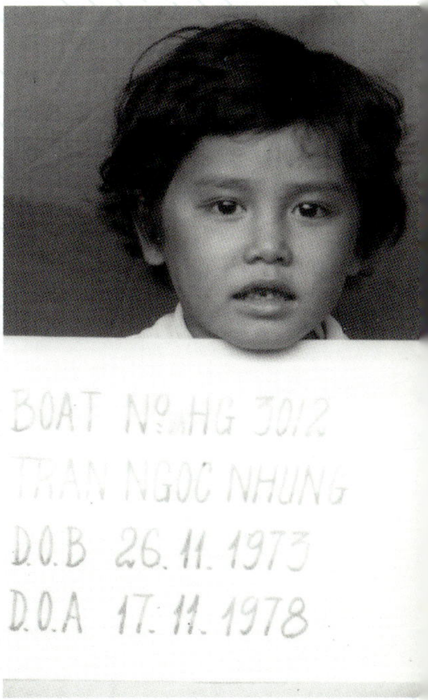

An identification photograph taken of Nhung when she was just five years old at a refugee camp in Malaysia.
NHUNG N. TRAN-DAVIES

we had little freedom of movement, and food was scarce. We were often desperate to find even a grain of rice to eat. People were being robbed and killed for a bag of rice. What little food we had was rationed by the government, but the rations were never enough for all of us."

Eventually conditions grew unbearably difficult, as Nhung's mother could not find enough work as a seamstress to provide for everyone. "Our mom saw no future for us in this war-ravaged land, especially after our home was flooded in a storm. Our family was stuck living in the little loft of our hut," Nhung tells me. "Mom knew then that if there was going to be hope for her children, it lay beyond the sea. Like many loving parents, she sacrificed everything to take us out to sea in search of a better future."

Nhung and her family boarded a boat and left everything they knew in Vietnam behind. They landed on the shores of Malaysia and lived in a refugee camp, with many other families who were hoping to start a new life. "Because I was five then, I can remember only glimpses of our life there. I remember waiting in line to get our rations of food from the Red Cross. There was a bun with sweet butter that I can still remember savoring to this day," Nhung says. "We had to build our own shelter in the camp, and my older siblings, especially my then 15-year-old brother, will probably never forget what happened when he was trying to chop some wood. Without his knowledge, I stood behind him, and when he lifted the ax to cut the wood, he accidentally cut me instead, on the left cheek. I still have the scar!"

While at this camp the Tran family received the news that they would be resettling in Canada, and soon they boarded an airplane headed for Edmonton. As Nhung remembers, the younger children in her family adapted more quickly. "It was easy for me to make friends, and it helped that there were a few other Vietnamese refugee kids starting [school] at the same time. What I didn't particularly enjoy were the harsh winters," she tells me. "My older sister had to piggyback me through some of the deep snow to get to school. Some of us hid inside the school when there was outdoor recess."

The dislike of snow and frigid temperatures affected the adults too, who feared their children would fall seriously ill. "The teachers in Edmonton had to get used to us sometimes coming to school smelling like tiger balm, as our parents slathered us in it each time we got sick. The teachers also had to learn that our parents weren't trying to hurt us when we showed up at school with red 'coining' marks on our necks and backs. It was just a traditional Vietnamese medical approach our parents had subjected us to so we could get well."

Eventually Nhung went to medical school and became a physician, but she never forgot her roots. She founded the Children of Vietnam Benevolent Foundation and spoke at the United Nations' International Organization on Migration in

Nhung's family boarded a boat and left Vietnam as refugees in 1979. KATERYNA.SOKOLOVA/ SHUTTERSTOCK.COM

Nhung's family had a hard time adapting to the harsh winters in Edmonton, AB. WENDY NERO/ SHUTTERSTOCK.COM

Geneva as part of their "I Am a Migrant" campaign, intended to help reduce hate speech and promote tolerance. She is a mother now, with three young children. I ask her what she tries to teach them about her past as a refugee.

"When I see our children taking for granted what they have, I remind them of the sacrifices their grandma made and where we come from—the war and poverty. It is my hope that they will always remember where we come from so that they grow with hearts full of gratitude, humility and kindness," she explains. "As well, I hope for them to not only have compassion and empathy for those who become refugees, but also knowledge of the horrors of war. I want them to know that humanity can do better."

I ask Nhung—a successful doctor, advocate, author and mother—what she loves most about her life in Canada now. "I love our life in Canada because this is a land of hope and opportunities. It gives me great comfort to know that my children can become whatever they want to be if they work hard enough. I love the peace and the beauty of our diverse terrains from coast to coast. I also love the people of Canada—our diverse colors, cultural background and history. And yet we share a common heart that wants to make our world a better place."

Nhung's extended family gathers for a photo in Alberta, Canada.
NHUNG N. TRAN-DAVIES

efugee and migrant children from many different countries play outside a learning center in Istanbul, Turkey. In 2020, Turkey hosted the largest number of refugees in the world. CHRIS MCGRATH/GETTY IMAGES

Saul's
OPEN 7 DAYS
DELICATESSEN
SANDWICHES · GROCERIES · COFFEE
OPEN
OPEN
ATM
LOTTO
KI

Three

Racism and Hardship

Immigration brings people from all over the world to live in the same place. In New York City, one of the most diverse places in the world, 40 percent of residents were born outside the United States. In London, England, the two most commonly spoken languages (other than English) are Bengali and Polish. In Sydney, Australia, the Nepalese and Lebanese communities are quickly growing.

However, immigration sometimes makes some longer-term residents uncomfortable as they see businesses changing to serve the needs of newcomers, or hear different languages being spoken on the streets or on the bus. This discomfort can grow into racism, which is when someone discriminates against a group of people because of their race, culture, religion or place of birth. Racism can affect governments too, and policies that adversely affect immigrants, refugees and Indigenous Peoples can be shaped according to prejudices against those groups.

New York City is one of the most diverse cities in the world. Almost 800 different languages are spoken there.
IMAGE SOURCE/GETTY IMAGES

Migration Facts

In 1907 an organization called the Asiatic Exclusion League, which opposed immigration from Asian countries, sparked a riot in Vancouver, British Columbia's Chinatown and Japantown, causing damage to Asian-owned businesses.

HISTORY OF ANTI-IMMIGRATION POLICY

Thomas Jefferson, the third president of the United States, was a powerful and influential leader, one of the men credited with the birth of the United States as a country. He was one of the authors of the Declaration of Independence, which declared that the United States was no longer under British rule. He often wrote about equality and human rights. But he also bought, sold and owned Black slaves. At his plantation in Virginia, called Monticello, he owned more than 600 slaves and is believed to have had children with one of them, a woman named Sally Hemings. While other early leaders of the United States, such as Ben Franklin and George Washington, later called for an end to slavery, Jefferson continued to view slaves as essential to the building of the country, writing that Black people could "save the expense of white settlers" and that Blacks were "pests in society." He believed in slavery for the entirety of his adult life and advocated for its benefits.

During his lifetime, Thomas Jefferson, the third president of the United States, owned more than 600 slaves at his plantation in Virginia. Some of the families had been under his ownership for four generations.
HULTON ARCHIVE/GETTY IMAGES

Alfred Deakin (far right) brought in Australia's Immigration Restriction Act. It restricted nonwhite and non-British immigrants from coming to the country. HULTON ARCHIVE/GETTY IMAGES

When he died in 1826, the start of the American Civil War was still 35 years in the future, and slavery would not end until the war ended in 1865. Slavery's long existence, and the continued racism against Black Americans, is partly due to Thomas Jefferson's power to influence policy with his own racist views.

In 1901 Australia's attorney general, Alfred Deakin, who would later be elected prime minister, introduced the Immigration Restriction Act, which almost totally cut off immigration from non-European countries. It was, in fact, informally called the "White Australia Policy," and was built on Deakin's own distaste for, in his words, "all alien colored immigration." The policy's racism, which became impossible to enforce as labor shortages pushed Australia to accept immigrants from other countries after World War II, is still visible today with the anti-Asian and anti-Muslim sentiments communicated by the Australia First Party, whose platform is based on stopping immigration from certain countries.

As you can see, the fact that racism affects government programs and systems is not new. From the policies meant to discourage immigrants from China to North America in the early 20th century to the British National Party today, whose members are publicly against immigration, to the

Moving On

On November 9–10, 1938, under the secret directions of the Nazi Party, protesters destroyed and vandalized synagogues and Jewish-owned businesses in Germany, Austria and Czechoslovakia, and agents imprisoned some 30,000 Jewish men, most of whom were later transported to concentration camps. This night is known as Kristallnacht, or Night of Broken Glass.

restrictions on migrants and refugees that the United States is putting into place right now, these policies change as attitudes about different groups of people change.

WHY ARE PEOPLE AGAINST IMMIGRANTS?

The economy

As you learned in chapter 1, one of the reasons countries want immigrants is so they can get inexpensive labor. This is especially true when a country is growing physically or economically. For example, in the 1990s Ireland welcomed large numbers of immigrants from many different countries because its economy was growing quickly, led by tech companies that specialized in developing computer- and internet-related products and services. During boom times, immigrant workers are often needed to keep the growth going.

Eventually, though, a country will stop growing. The number of available jobs will decrease, and some people will

be unemployed and have less money to spend. When this occurs, immigrants and refugees are often blamed, especially if they are visibly different because of skin color or religious clothing such as hijabs, turbans or yarmulkes. If such people are working and own homes in their new country, people who were born there might think that jobs and housing are less available to them because of the newcomers.

Unemployment and poverty depend on many factors that are unrelated to immigration, including whether a government funds programs that help create jobs, what products are being bought and sold between countries, and political conflict. Immigrants not only fill existing jobs but also create jobs, starting their own businesses and employing people to work for them. They spend money at stores and use services such as schools and hospitals, activities that also provide jobs. A country's economic history is never simple.

Alan Ramadan, a refugee from Syria, attends a job-training program as an industrial mechanic in Germany. ALEXANDER KOERNER/GETTY IMAGES

Moving On

With Canada at war with both Germany and Japan during World War II, tensions ran high in its diverse communities. During this time more than 22,000 Japanese immigrants and Japanese Canadians were removed from coastal British Columbia by the Canadian government and relocated to internment camps inland, where they stayed until the war was over. In 1988 then prime minister Brian Mulroney made an official apology to the internment survivors, who also received a $300-million compensation package.

Current world events

Racism against immigrants also occurs because of current world events. If a war or terrorist attack involves a person or persons from a specific place in the world, people may believe that everyone in that community has the same views and is capable of the same kind of violence.

Perhaps the most famous example of this is what happened after the attack in the United States on September 11, 2001. On that day two airplanes crashed into the World Trade Center in New York City and one into the Pentagon in Washington, DC, killing almost 3,000 people. The airplanes had been hijacked (taken over from the pilots and crew) by people working for al-Qaeda, an organization that considers the United States an enemy of the Islamic faith. It's important to note that Islam is a religion with millions of nonviolent followers, while al-Qaeda is an extremist group that uses religion to incite violence. Islam itself, like any religion, is mostly embraced by people to help guide their lives in peaceful, daily ways.

After the attacks, people blamed Islam and the people who follow that religion, who are called Muslims. Across the United States, mosques were vandalized—in some cases they were set on fire. People who appeared to be Middle Eastern or spoke with an accent were harassed in public. Even today anti-Muslim racism continues worldwide. According to the American Civil Liberties Union, anti-mosque incidents have occurred in 44 out of 50 states since 2005. Similar incidents have occurred in Birmingham, England; Quebec City, Canada; and Christchurch, New Zealand. In 2017 President Donald Trump issued a travel ban, barring people from seven Muslim-majority countries from entering the United States.

Acts of violence and hatred are committed by individuals. They are not committed by all members of a racial or religious group. It is important to remember that the people responsible for acts of war or terrorism represent only a small percentage of the communities they come from. Most people don't start wars—they simply want to be able to live in peace and safety.

A vigil for victims of the shooting attacks on al-Noor and Linwood mosques in Christchurch, New Zealand.
CAM MCLAREN/GETTY IMAGES

Sudden migration

In 1992 the European Union (EU) was formed officially by Belgium, France, Germany, Denmark, Greece, Ireland, Italy, Great Britain, Luxembourg, the Netherlands, Portugal and Spain. This union created political alliances and made travel and trade simpler across borders. It also ensured that people could move and work more freely between European countries. In the following years, as more nations in eastern Europe joined the EU, people from those countries began to travel westward. Between 2004 and 2014, 1.5 million people from Cyprus, the Czech Republic, Estonia, Hungary, Latvia, Lithuania, Malta, Poland, Slovakia and Slovenia settled in the United Kingdom, looking for better jobs and education. This huge migration of people in a relatively short time was a big change for the British people, as the country had not seen that much immigration in its history. Many people felt uneasy with how their society was changing so quickly. *Hate crimes*—crimes that harass or assault people because of their race, culture, sexuality or religion—against people from eastern Europe have been reported more and more in the media in recent years. In 2016 the United Kingdom held a referendum on whether to leave the EU, and the yes side won. Many people believe that citizens were voting against immigration and diversity.

This racism occurs when people who have lived somewhere for a long time see their country changing, and are afraid they will no longer feel comfortable there or will lose career or education opportunities. The fear of outsiders or anything foreign is called *xenophobia*. For most people, getting to know their new neighbors and finding common interests will ease their worries and help them see that all people, no matter where they're from, share the same goals of finding safety, happiness and peace. Some people, however, resent the newcomers and express that resentment. Racism can be as obvious as painting insults on the walls of a mosque, or it can be less visible. For example, someone with

Migration Facts

In 2016 the majority of immigrants to Australia were from India and China, a marked difference from just 10 years earlier, when most newcomers were from the United Kingdom.

Immigrants want the same thing as everybody else—a home where they feel safe, happy and healthy.
TAIYOU NOMACHI/GETTY IMAGES

Xenophobia is the fear of people, such as immigrants, who may not speak the same language or wear the same type of clothes as other people in a community.
FATCAMERA/GETTY IMAGES

a name that sounds Sikh may not get hired for a job. They will likely never know if it was because of racism, but it could be, even though that kind of discrimination is technically illegal in most places. There are many reasons people fear or resent immigrants, reasons that are often based on personal experience and specific concerns.

Unfamiliarity with culture

The transition to a diverse society is a challenging one, and it's something that has occurred throughout history. Perhaps one of the biggest reasons people resent immigrants is that they are unfamiliar with the newcomers' culture and fear the ways it is different from their own. Anti-Islam racism, which is widespread, is often related to how many people in the Western world do not understand some of Islam's visible cultural traditions. Many Muslim women, for example, cover their hair with hijabs (head scarves) and dress modestly, arms and legs covered. It is easy to misunderstand this tradition. After all, in North America and

Europe we are used to women dressing however they like. In some Muslim-majority countries, women must cover their heads (and often their faces) by law, but in others women choose to wear the coverings as a sign of their faith. When these women emigrate to other countries, they wear hijabs or niqabs (veils) by choice, and doing so gives them a connection to their culture and religion.

People sometimes think these women are made to cover their hair and that Islamic religion and culture force rules on people, whether they like them or not. But this isn't always true. All religions provide rules for people to live by. Those rules could be about covering your hair or about waiting until marriage to have sex or about how often to pray. It's true that there are extremist groups within every religion, and those groups often interpret their religion in ways that oppress or abuse others. However, making judgments about an entire religion, race or culture based on one visible difference is misinformed and can lead to racism. Everyone's culture, even yours, is unfamiliar to people in other countries.

Moving On

Marriage and relationships between Black Americans and white Americans were illegal in several American states from the late 1600s onward. In 1900, 26 states had what were called anti-miscegenation laws. In 1967 the Supreme Court ruled that these state laws were unconstitutional. It wasn't until 2000 that the last state, Alabama, eliminated its laws against interracial marriage.

A mother and her son arrive at a mosque in London on the last day of Ramadan.
DAN KITWOOD/GETTY IMAGES

Migration Facts

Every year over 700,000 people from other countries become citizens of the United States. Two hundred thousand become citizens of Canada. In 2018 more than 80,000 people became Australian citizens.

WHY ARE PEOPLE AGAINST REFUGEES?

Many of the reasons people are against refugees are the same reasons they are against immigrants. However, there are a couple of reasons that are unique to refugees and what they represent.

Fear of crime

There are over 25 million refugees worldwide, all of whom are looking for a safe place to live. They come from Syria, Myanmar, South Sudan, Guatemala, Honduras and many other countries. In these countries, war, gang violence and rebel fighting have forced families to flee in large numbers, often crossing borders in groups of as many as 1,000 people.

In 2018 several groups of asylum seekers left Central America and arrived in Mexico. By 2019, 6,000 people have left their homes on foot to try to reach safety in the

More than 2,000 young children were part of the Central American migrant caravan in 2018. SPENCER PLATT/GETTY IMAGES

United States, only to be turned away. The United States has deployed extra troops to ports of entry, fired tear gas at migrants attempting to cross the border and threatened to cut off foreign aid to Central American governments unless they start to help manage the waves of migrants. In Mexico, since January 2019, more than 80,000 migrants have been detained and then deported, while others have been denied humanitarian visas or left waiting in poorly equipped camps.

Honduran migrants were part of the caravan to the Mexico–United States border. VIC HINTERLANG/ SHUTTERSTOCK.COM

Some asylum seekers enter countries by paying criminal organizations to help them get there. Sometimes seekers have criminal records in their home countries because they were child soldiers, or they stole money or food to survive, or they protested against an unfair government.

For these reasons people can be afraid that terrorists or criminals are using the refugee system to enter a country, where they will then commit violent crimes. However, the refugee claim process, which happens when an asylum seeker is asked to provide evidence that their claim is legitimate, is designed to assess any security risks an individual might represent. For the most part, refugees are simply people escaping hardship and looking to settle in a country that is safe.

Migration Facts

Every year about 96,000 international students come to Canada to study.

Cost

When large numbers of asylum seekers are making refugee claims, it may seem that dealing with them involves a huge cost. After all, it takes a lot of effort to provide housing, food and healthcare for groups of people who arrive in a country suddenly. Worries about the cost to taxpayers and the strain on government services can turn into racist resentment, with people using the cost as a reason to deny a proper refugee-claim process, something that everyone in the world has the right to ask for. But funding for refugees can come from many sources. It can be fully funded by the government or by the government in cooperation with a sponsor—an individual or group that offers financial and other supports to a particular refugee or refugee family. Or refugees can be entirely funded by a sponsor, with no ***resettlement*** costs to the government at all.

In 2018, Canada resettled 28,000 refugees, the most of any country in the world.
JASMIN MERDAN/GETTY IMAGES

Accepting refugees is a *humanitarian* act, an initiative a country can take to help people who would otherwise be at risk of injury, torture or death in their home countries. Through refugee programs, receiving countries reduce the risk of war and genocide, which is when a government or group tries to eradicate an entire community of people, usually through violence. There is no doubt that accepting refugees costs a lot of money, but it is also an investment in a safer future for vulnerable people.

RUQUYA AL-ITBI

Home Is More Than One Place

In 2015, when Ruquya Al-itbi was 10 years old, she, her younger sister, Narjis, and their parents fled Baghdad, the capital city of Iraq, and traveled to Pattaya, Thailand. There they waited for four years as their refugee claim was processed, and in that time they began to settle into a new family routine. A third daughter, Fatema, was born. Ruquya and Narjis attended an international school, where they learned Arabic, English, Thai and Chinese. In Thailand, away from the political instability and lack of educational opportunities for women in Iraq, Ruquya felt at home. "Pattaya is a really cool place," she says. "It's hot. It's fun. All my friends are there."

Ruquya exceled at school in Pattaya and developed close friendships with her classmates. Even though she always knew her family was not planning on staying in Thailand, she couldn't help but wish they could. She remembers vividly how she felt when her parents told her in late 2018 that they would be moving permanently to Canada as refugees. "I just cried. My friends told me, 'Why don't you come to our house and tell your mom and dad that you will never go to Canada?' " she tells me. "And one of my teachers, who doesn't have any babies, said to my parents, 'I'm going

Ruquya in Pattaya, Thailand, where she and her family waited to be resettled.
RUQUYA AL-ITBI

Ruquya and her family.
RUQUYA AL-ITBI

Ruquya Al-itbi in Kelowna, BC.
RUQUYA AL-ITBI

to adopt Ruquya. She's going to be my daughter. Just don't go to Canada.' I cried. I hated my life. It was so bad."

After arriving in Vancouver in 2019, the family moved to Kelowna, British Columbia, where Ruquya, despite her doubts, found herself welcomed by her school and community. When she started ninth grade at her middle school, it was a happy beginning. "My school is the best school ever," she explains. "I just came to school on the first day and everyone was like, 'Welcome to Canada!' It was really nice." Ruquya already has a close and diverse group of friends. "One of my friends, she's from Mexico, and the other from Spain, and the other is Canadian, and the other one from China. It's really fun. And the Canadians are really nice!"

Ruquya plans to take advantage of the education that is available to her in Canada and become an engineer. Eventually she hopes to return to and work in Thailand, which she misses daily. "I feel like someone is eating my heart or cutting my heart," she explains. "My heart is half in Thailand and half with me." Her sisters, now 10 and 3 years old, love their lives in Canada, and this gives Ruquya a lot of comfort. "They really love Canada," she tells me. "They want to live here forever!"

For now Ruquya stays in online contact with her friends in Thailand while she forges ahead in her new city and new school. Like many refugees, Ruquya's idea of home is ever shifting. But it will always mean more than just one place.

MARIANA VEIGA

The Search for Opportunity and Safety

In 1996, when Mariana Veiga was 14 years old, she and her parents and younger brother moved from Rio de Janeiro, Brazil, to Vancouver, Canada. Her mother, a metals and mineral engineer, had begun a postdoctoral fellowship at the University of British Columbia, studying nuclear energy. Mariana's father, a mining engineer, was hired at the same university to teach and to research mercury contamination. After packing up their lives and saying goodbye to their large extended family, the family settled in Vancouver, staying at first in faculty housing on the large landscaped campus.

For Mariana, the early days in Canada felt like a dream. "The faculty housing there is almost like a closed community," she remembers. "It's houses and low-rise buildings, all designed for pedestrians. For a kid, it's like paradise! People were riding bikes and playing hockey outside or walking to the neighbor's house." This sense of safety and freedom was new to Mariana and her family, who had come from crowded Rio de Janeiro, where class inequality contributes to the number of families and neighborhoods that struggle with poverty. "In Brazil, if you work at a coffee shop, you're not going to make ends meet," Mariana explains. "A lot of people who live in the slums work. They have little brick houses or wooden shacks. They work at restaurants

In 1996 Mariana Veiga's family left Rio de Janeiro, Brazil, for Vancouver, BC.
PHOTO COKADA/GETTY IMAGES

and coffee shops, and the salaries are so bad. People don't get paid very much for labor."

Mariana and her oldest son, Rafael.
MARIANA VEIGA

Her parents, Mariana says, "were looking for a better life, more stability in terms of education, healthcare, more opportunities for the kids. When you grow up in a country that's not safe, your radar is always on. When you're walking down the street, you're always attentive to what's going on around you." In Canada her parents felt that their children could play where they wanted, study what they wanted and pursue any job that interested them.

When Mariana started high school in Vancouver, a city famous for its diversity, she was fascinated by how so many of the students had roots in other countries. "My friends were all international. I had one Canadian friend, the rest from all over the world. I had never met people from those areas, those parts of the world. I thought that was really cool. One of my good friends in high school was from Iran, one was from Afghanistan, one was from Germany. These were places I didn't know!"

Even as Mariana grew to love Vancouver, she also missed her family and old home. "I still miss the food, the beaches, the people, the sunshine," she tells me. "My parents made a point to take me back at least every other year to see family. Now all my grandparents have passed away, so I don't know when will be the next time. I still want to keep that connection. I want my kids to see my roots and where I'm from and to see how beautiful Brazil is."

Now a nurse, Mariana is married to Mauricio, himself an immigrant to Canada from Bogotá, Colombia, and they have three young sons, Rafael, Leonardo and Diego. Maintaining ties to both of their cultures is a priority. Every Sunday the family attends a Portuguese community-center program with activities that help the children learn the language and the traditions of Brazil. "I just want to transfer a little bit of culture to my kids," Mariana explains.

Global cultural knowledge is important to Mariana and Mauricio. "I want my kids to embrace cultures, diversity, and be knowledgeable about the world," she says. "And I don't know if I think that because I'm an immigrant. I had the opportunity to travel a fair amount with my parents, and that chance grew exponentially when we were in Canada. There were so many more opportunities. I want my kids to have the opportunity to be open-minded, to embrace the diversity and cultures of the world. This is my biggest thing."

As our conversation draws to a close, Mariana tells me a story that she has just remembered about her grandmother and the distance between them after her family immigrated. "My grandma came here two years ago for my brother's wedding," she recalls, "and she actually passed away here while she was visiting. It was the first time all her children and grandchildren were together in six years." Mariana believes it was her grandmother's greatest wish to see all of her family together one last time. "And she passed away three days after my brother's wedding. Isn't that crazy?"

Mariana, Mauricio, Rafael and Leonardo Veiga maintain ties to their Brazilian and Colombian cultures.
MARIANA VEIGA

SAMER MUSCATI

A Lifelong Advocate for Refugees

Samer Muscati is a human-rights lawyer who has lived all over the world, working to protect the rights of people scarred and displaced by armed conflict. Samer is the director of the International Human Rights Program at the University of Toronto Faculty of Law, where his work focuses on women's rights, refugee rights and children with disabilities. He is also a former journalist and photographer—many of his photographs of people in post-conflict countries have been exhibited in art shows across Canada. Samer is the father of twin girls, Zadie and Mika, and is married to Sandra Ka Hon Chu, also a human-rights lawyer and (full disclosure!) my best friend.

Two young girls, one with albinism, in Mozambique, one of the areas Samer has researched and photographed working with Human Rights Watch.
SAMER MUSCATI

Because Samer has dedicated his life to helping people who have been displaced, I want to talk with him about what working in refugee rights is really like and what has to happen to force people to flee their homes. "In my experience, nobody wants to leave their world behind, their family, friends, house, possessions, basically their entire life, unless they absolutely have to," he explains. "One of the most difficult things imaginable is choosing all the things you can fit into a bag, saying goodbye to your loved ones without any sense of whether you will see them again and then heading to a foreign land that you've never seen before. Often it's not a choice—it's either flee or perish."

Samer has traveled to many countries and spent time with displaced people in Syria, Iraq, South Sudan and Nigeria. Much of his work focuses on helping women and girls. "Displacement has a huge effect on families and children, girls in particular," he tells me. "Oftentimes mothers with their children are separated from the father when fleeing. During times of conflict women and girls face increasing levels of violence, including rape, trafficking, abduction and early marriage. Women are often the last to flee their homes and towns, as they usually ensure the safety of family members before their own. Those who make it out safely are still at risk of abuse because the sole responsibility for acquiring food, wood and water for their families rests on their shoulders. During crises, families are more likely to pull their girls out of school, and those girls are less likely to return than boys." What women need to do to protect their children is an enormous weight, but it also makes them activists and survivors. As Samer puts it, "Despite all of this, women still manage to be the glue that holds communities and families together."

A young migrant girl at the Piraeus port in Greece.
ALEXANDROS MICHAILIDIS/SHUTTERSTOCK.COM

Looking back on his career, he says the experience of interviewing Yazidi women and girls who had escaped ISIS (the radical Islamic group) in Syria continues to haunt him. "They had lost everything, including their families. I remember in particular one girl who really resembled one of my teenaged cousins back home in Ottawa, and that made it more difficult for me to process the cruelty and trauma that these women and girls had to endure and continue to endure."

As a father Samer focuses on making sure his children understand what refugees survive. "I think kids should know that refugees are incredibly brave people who have endured some of the hardest things a person could ever endure," he says. "They are tenacious, and they are survivors. And at the end of the day, they are just like any one of us seeking a life free from violence and oppression for themselves and their families."

When I ask what he wants his daughters to know about war and displacement, he says, "I plan to teach the twins to acknowledge their own extraordinary privilege of having been born and raised in a country not at war. We collectively have a responsibility to challenge the roots of the worst human rights crises—imperialism, colonialism, racism and capitalism—and to acknowledge that our privilege is born from and often reinforces other people's oppression. I hope to teach them to use that privilege to help their brothers and sisters around the world."

Haja, a longtime activist, flashes the peace sign on the eve of Libya's first democratic election in 2012.
SAMER MUSCATI

The Akcakale refugee camp in Turkey. It's home to approximately 28,000 Syrian refugees.
TOLGA SEZGIN/SHUTTERSTOCK.COM

Four

Life in a New Country

What is life as an immigrant or refugee really like? We often see news footage of refugees or immigrants arriving, but we know very little of their lives after they have settled in their new homes. In this chapter you'll learn what happens in the months and years after migrants move to a different country and about what the future holds.

The first Syrian refugees arrived at Toronto's Pearson International Airport in 2015.
STACEY NEWMAN/GETTY IMAGES

CHALLENGES

Building a brand-new life in a different country is a lot of hard work. Immigrants and refugees often need help settling in, and immigrant-support organizations provide them with guidance so that their lives can be happy and secure. When my grandfather first arrived in Canada, he relied on the free English classes that were offered at the local church in Chinatown, as well as the support of Lee's Benevolent Association, one of many family associations that helped Chinese immigrants find jobs, fill out government forms and make friends. Here are some of the challenges that immigrants face and need help with.

The Sri Lankan civil war ended in 2009. Hundreds of thousands of people were displaced during the 25-year war.
ALLISON JOYCE/GETTY IMAGES

Racism

One of the biggest challenges of moving to a different country is the racism an immigrant might face. When people arrive from a country that has been at war, which is commonly the case with refugees seeking asylum, people in the new country often have little understanding of the conflict the refugees have left behind. For example, when the ships carrying asylum seekers from Sri Lanka arrived on the west coast of Canada in 2010, some of the public discussion was focused on whether these asylum seekers were terrorists. There had been little media coverage in Canada about the Sri Lankan civil war, and it was easy for people to make assumptions with scant information. In the wake of the terrorist attacks of September 11, 2001, some people became afraid of anyone from countries in the Middle East or South Asia.

Migration Facts

More than 200 languages are spoken in Australia.

Getting a job

Many immigrants (and some refugees) move to other countries in order to find a secure job. When people's homelands have been destabilized by war or a government in turmoil, employment becomes difficult to obtain and keep. In their new homes, one of their main goals is to find a job that enables them to support themselves and their families. However, it can be difficult to find work. Sometimes immigrants are not yet fluent in the language of the new country, making communication during a job interview or in a work setting challenging. The training or education someone received in their home country often isn't recognized in their new home. For example, certification in fields such as healthcare, engineering, medicine, law and teaching is highly regulated. And it can be a daunting task to look for work in a country whose systems—like income tax, social security and unions—are unfamiliar. Some employers might prefer to hire people who don't need help figuring out those details.

Migration Facts

More than 500,000 refugees in Africa are in need of a permanent home, but there are only 18,000 resettlement spaces.

A refugee from Pakistan attends a job-training program for electrical engineers in Garbsen, Germany.
ALEXANDER KOERNER/GETTY IMAGES

Learning a new language

When settling into a different country, immigrants and refugees often have to learn a new language in order to get jobs, go to school or make friends. Immersion in a new language is often easier for children because their brains and language skills are still developing. For adults this is a longer process, and it can be particularly difficult for stay-at-home parents who don't use the language every day in a workplace. The good news is that settlement-support agencies help newcomers find language classes that suit their schedules and fluency levels, as language really is the first step in making a home in a different country.

Generational conflict

Taking on the culture of a new country is something children and young people prioritize more than adults do. Adults who immigrate often bring with them the traditions of their home countries. These can involve clothing, food, religion and rules about dating and marriage. Holding on to these traditions combats feelings of loneliness or homesickness, helping adults feel more comfortable. But their children, who go to school every day and are immersed in popular culture, music, social media and customs, may have trouble applying their parents' traditions to their lives. For example, the custom of families choosing whom their children will marry is more difficult to manage in a country where dating and romance are seen as the only ways to find a partner. Conflicting cultural traditions can cause real divisions in families, particularly when they are ones that affect everyone in the family, practically and emotionally. For many families, finding support from other members of their communities, through a faith-based group or settlement

Food is one way immigrants stay connected to their culture in a new country.
KATE_SEPT2004/GETTY IMAGES

Moving On

Immigrants always bring their home country's food with them to their new homes, and inevitably the dishes change over time, becoming a fusion of old and new. Some examples include mulligatawny, a soup brought to England from South India that is now commonly seen in English pubs and restaurants, chop suey, a type of stir-fry believed to have originated with Chinese cooks who worked during the construction of the Canadian and American railroads, and rijsttafel, a rice dish with spiced vegetables and meats, which was brought to the Netherlands by Indonesian immigrants.

agency, can really help. It is hugely comforting to know that other families have survived these conflicts and can help with advice and support.

BENEFITS

Moving to a new country is hard, especially if you arrive with little money and cannot speak the language. But there are also many positive things about being an immigrant. My father, who arrived in Canada at age 15 to join his father, lived in two different worlds. One was the English-speaking Canadian world he participated in at school and with his friends, where he styled his hair like Elvis Presley and fell in love with movie musicals like *Singin' in the Rain*. The other was the Cantonese-speaking world of his parents and Chinatown, where people ate wonton noodle soup for lunch and played xiangqi (a board game similar to chess) at the local diner. For my father, there were a lot of benefits in being able to be in one world and then the other, to learn that cultures can be different but still co-exist and that one

It can be exciting and scary to move to a new country.
THIANCHAI SITTHIKONGSAK/GETTY IMAGES

isn't better than the other. My father was an outgoing person, and his ease in traveling between languages and cultures later made him a community leader who helped recent immigrants with their taxes and government forms.

The opportunity to explore a new culture

Moving and trying to understand a new culture can be overwhelming, especially when you're also trying to find a job or a home. However, being immersed in a different culture can also be really exciting. Can you think of a time you traveled to another country on vacation, and how fun it was to try new foods and explore? Immigration is a learning experience every day.

Meeting people from different places

Most of the countries that people move to, including Canada, the United States and Australia, are diverse places—countries

Moving On

At the 2016 Summer Olympics in Rio de Janeiro, Brazil, 10 athletes made up the first-ever Refugee Olympic Team:

- Yusra Mardini, Syria, 100-meter freestyle swim
- Yiech Pur Biel, South Sudan, 800-meter run
- Rami Anis, Syria, 100-meter butterfly swim
- Yonas Kinde, Ethiopia, marathon
- Anjelina Nadai Lohalith, South Sudan, 1,500-meter run
- Rose Nathike Lokonyen, South Sudan, 800-meter run, team flag bearer
- James Nyang Chiengjiek, South Sudan, 400-meter run
- Paulo Amotun Lokoro, South Sudan, 1,500-meter run
- Popole Misenga, Democratic Republic of Congo, middleweight judo
- Yolande Bukasa Mabika, Democratic Republic of Congo, middleweight judo

Toronto's annual Caribana festival attracts over one million visitors a year.
REIMAR/SHUTTERSTOCK.COM

Migration Facts

Most immigrants to the United States come from Mexico.

whose residents come from all over the world. In 2016, 73 percent of people who lived in Scarborough, Ontario, a suburb of Toronto, were visible minorities. Not only can an immigrant family find a community from their home country, but they can also make connections with people from many other places and experience a diversity that may not have been possible in their country of origin. This can be a great learning opportunity and a way to just have fun. With diversity come cultural celebrations like Diwali, Caribana and Passover, events that anyone can participate in. Everyone loves a celebration with delicious food!

Different opportunities for work and education

When people leave their homes because of war or a lack of job opportunities, they usually immigrate to a place where there are good jobs, plenty of schools and security. For example, only 23 percent of teenage refugees in camps or temporary housing attend high school, while 84 percent of teenagers worldwide are enrolled in school. Moving to a country with good public schools, which indicates that education there is a priority, means refugees and immigrants will be better prepared to get good jobs.

Bringing your culture to your new country

In 2016 a group of Syrian women who had recently moved to Vancouver, British Columbia, hosted a refugee fund-raising dinner they called Tayybeh, which is the Arabic word for "delicious" and "kind." From offering monthly pop-up dinners the organization has grown into a popular catering company serving Syrian food such as falafel (deep-fried chickpea fritters), kibbeh (specially spiced meatballs) and namoura (sweet cakes topped with coconut). This kind of sharing, through food, art or other types of culture, adds diversity to a multicultural society and helps the people who live around you understand where you come from and how your family lives. And this, above all else, helps people build friendships and feel at home in their new countries.

Moving On

In 2018 the United Nations General Assembly adopted the Global Compact on Refugees and the Global Compact for Safe, Orderly and Regular Migration. Both compacts seek to protect the safety of migrants and refugees, particularly women and children, and establish international protocols for managing mass migration.

IMMIGRANTS AND REFUGEES IN THE SPOTLIGHT

The best way to find out what it's like to live as an immigrant or refugee is to talk to someone who has experienced it. Or you can read the stories of immigrants who have traveled across the globe to rebuild their lives. Following are profiles of people you may have heard of who are also immigrants or refugees.

JAMIE MCCARTHY/GETTY IMAGES

Malala Yousafzai was born in 1997 in Mingora, Pakistan, where her father, Ziauddin, ran an all-girls' school. When the Taliban (an Islamic extremist group that implemented strict rules and opposed education for women and girls) took control of their community in 2008, her father's school was forced to close. Malala and her father became outspoken advocates for universal education and publicly opposed Taliban rule. In 2012, on the way home from classes that were held in a secret location, Malala was shot in the head. She fell into a coma and spent her recovery in Birmingham, England, where her family eventually settled as refugees. In 2014 she was the youngest-ever recipient of the Nobel Peace Prize, and she has traveled all over the world, speaking about education and female empowerment. Today she is a student at the University of Oxford and she runs the Malala Fund, a charity that helps girls safely attend and finish 12 years of school.

DIMITRIOS KAMBOURIS/GETTY IMAGES

K'naan, whose real name is Keinan Abdi Warsame, is a Canadian rapper and hip-hop musician. His family fled the Somali Civil War in 1991 when he was 13 years old, traveling first to the United States and later being granted refugee status in Toronto. K'naan is now an accomplished musician whose song "Wavin' Flag," based on his childhood as a refugee, was used as the official anthem of the 2010 FIFA World Cup. Winner of four Juno Awards, he has also written essays and one book for children, *When I Get Older: The Story Behind "Wavin' Flag."*

Albert Einstein, the famous scientist who won the Nobel Prize in Physics in 1921, was born in in 1879 in Württemberg, Germany, to Jewish parents. After moving with his family to Italy and Switzerland, he returned to Germany in 1914 to work at the University of Berlin as a professor. In 1933, alarmed by the rise of Nazism, Einstein renounced his German citizenship and immigrated to the United States, where he worked at Princeton University as a professor of theoretical physics. He became an American citizen in 1940 and has been awarded every scientific honor in the world. He died in 1955 in Princeton, New Jersey.

The **Dalai Lama** was born in Taktser, Amdo, in northeastern Tibet, with the name Lhamo Dhondup. At age two he was identified as the reincarnation of the 13th Dalai Lama, Thubten Gyatso, the spiritual and political leader of Tibet. Lhamo began his education as a Buddhist monk at the age of 6, and in 1950, at age 15, he became the 14th Dalai Lama. That same year China invaded Tibet, and, fearing assassination, the Dalai Lama fled to Dharamsala, in northern India, where he still lives with many of his followers. He has spent much of his life advocating for a free and independent Tibet, as well as for peace in the many areas of conflict around the world. A charismatic and sought-after public speaker, the Dalai Lama has traveled to 67 countries and has received 150 honorary degrees and prizes, including the 1989 Nobel Peace Prize.

He has authored or co-authored 110 books and is known for his interest in the connections between science and spirituality.

THEO WARGO/GETTY IMAGES

Alek Wek was born in Wau, South Sudan, in 1977, the seventh of nine children. After the death of her father in 1985, civil war broke out, and to escape the violence Alek fled with her siblings and mother to London, England, where they were accepted as refugees. At age 18, Alek enrolled as a student at the London College of Fashion. She was soon discovered by a modeling scout at a market. She rose to fame when she starred in music videos for Tina Turner and Janet Jackson, later becoming the first African cover model in *ELLE* magazine's history. In addition to modeling, Alek is a goodwill ambassador for the United Nations High Commission for Refugees and is the author of a bestselling memoir, *Alek: From Sudanese Refugee to International Supermodel.*

NEILSON BARNARD/GETTY IMAGES

Mila Kunis was born in Chernivtsi, Ukraine, in 1983, when it was still part of the Soviet Union. At age seven she and her family moved to Los Angeles, California, as religious refugees. In the Soviet Union her parents had experienced anti-Semitism (discrimination against Jews). Once in the United States, Mila's mother, who was a physics teacher, worked in a pharmacy, and her father, a mechanical engineer, became a taxi driver. At age nine Mila began acting to help with her English and shyness and was cast in her first commercial—for Barbie dolls—shortly afterward. She is best known for her role in *That '70s Show* and in the critically acclaimed film *Black Swan,* and as the voice of Meg Griffin in the animated series *Family Guy.*

Anish Kapoor was born in 1954 in Mumbai, India, and moved to London in the late 1970s to study art at the Hornsey College of Art and the Chelsea School of Art and Design. Anish became known for his large sculptures, which use materials such as limestone and concrete in innovative ways. Cities around the world display his outdoor sculptures as public art. *Cloud Gate*, perhaps his most famous, is in Chicago. It's a stainless steel structure that residents affectionately nicknamed The Bean for its seamless bean-like shape. Other sculptures can be found in New York, San Gimignano in Italy, London and Paris. Anish won the Turner Prize, was named a Commander of the British Empire and received a knighthood in 2013 for his services to the visual arts.

For most immigrants and refugees, surviving in their new home is their primary concern. They have to find stable housing and good jobs and enroll their children in school. Once they are settled, though, their lives unfold very much like anyone else's. Children graduate from high school and go on to university. Couples get married. Babies are born. People go on vacation and attend family and cultural celebrations. Even though their origins might not be the same as yours, immigrants and refugees are humans with families and feelings and ambitions, just like all of us.

OMAR AKUBAR

Social Worker, Teacher, Father, Refugee

When Omar Akubar and his family first arrived in Canada from Kenya in 2017, he remembers feeling a huge sense of surprise. "It was so cold!" he exclaims to me. "In Africa it's always hot. They have windy, they have sunny, they have rain. In Vancouver it was so cold! I couldn't see the sun. I was in shock!" With his wife, Bibi, and six children, he traveled to the small town of New Denver, British Columbia, where it was even colder. "When we went to New Denver everywhere was white—snow, all the roofs of the houses, all the people, everything was white. It was something unimaginable, incredible for us," he remembers. He knew right then that adapting to life in a new country was going to take some time.

Omar's journey to Canada began in 1999 when, as a young man, he left Somalia for Kenya, where he was classified as an asylum seeker. A member of a minority group known as the Somali Bantu, he left Somalia because of discrimination. The Bantu, who came to Somalia hundreds of years ago as slaves, are even now routinely treated poorly by ethnic Somalis, who are in positions of power in business, government and law enforcement.

Omar wasn't treated much better in Kenya. "There was harassment, also lack of respect," he explains. "I was not able to provide my children with education there. They have some free education, but they don't have quality." He soon realized that the Bantu were also discriminated against in Kenya, where he and others had difficulty navigating systems for asylum seekers. Frustrated with the lack of services for his people, Omar became a social worker and teacher, helping others who had fled Somalia find housing, jobs, education and healthcare. Eventually Omar built an entire life in Nairobi, gaining refugee status, meeting his wife and building his family of six children. "I think a lot about Kenya *and* Somalia," he tells me, "because both are countries where I came from. My second country is Kenya, because it's where I got married and made some money."

Omar with one of his sons in Edmonton, AB.
OMAR AKUBAR

As the years passed, Omar and Bibi saw that their children had few opportunities in Kenya. They applied to the United Nations Refugee Agency, which helped them resettle in Canada. After a short time in New Denver, the family moved permanently to Edmonton, Alberta, where they started to build a new life. They now have a home, and all the older children are enrolled in public school. "My favorite thing about living in Canada is how people really respect each other, how people have value in Canada," he reflects. "I like how they respect education. How the government offers free education for people with both low income and high income. This makes me happy." His children, whose opportunities were limited in Nairobi, are dreaming big dreams. "Everyone has ambitions. One of my sons wants to be a police officer, another one wants to be a pilot, another wants to be a doctor. My daughter also wants to be a nurse. 'Okay,' I tell them, 'work hard, don't always look at the TV. Study! Learn!' They are free to do whatever they like now. The option belongs to them."

Still, being a refugee in a different country has its challenges. It has been difficult for Omar to find work that fulfills him. "Newcomers have to build their position, their occupation, here," he says. "What they used to do they can't do here when they come. They have to go to school, they have to rebuild what they know again. Of course, you can get a job, but what you used to do you can't get. Unless you study a lot. I like to do things very quickly! So I can support my family and be an independent person." As he parents his children, taking them to activities and helping them with homework, he often thinks about what he misses about his old life in Nairobi. "I miss the community I used to work for," he tells me. "All the other refugees who were Somali like me. What I miss are all the services I used to do for them. I miss teaching my community and taking care of them. I miss what I used to do a long time ago."

Even with his challenges, Omar remains optimistic about the future, especially for his children. As he explains to me, the opportunities in Canada are endless because "Canadians respect and care, and they value you as a person."

AYELET TSABARI

From Israel to Canada and Back Again

In 1998 Ayelet Tsabari fell in love with a Canadian man and left her home in Tel Aviv, Israel, to live in Vancouver, British Columbia. She had visited many places all over the world already, including parts of the United States, Thailand and India, but it was Vancouver she ended up living in for over 20 years. "I was traveling a lot, so I don't know if it felt like such a monumental moment when I left for Canada. Also, I didn't know whether I'd stay or not. That's why I call myself an 'accidental immigrant,'" she explains. "The day I landed in Vancouver, it was June 21, the longest day of the year. The sun set at 9:45 p.m., and I'd never seen the sun set that late before. It was so surreal and disorienting and cool, seeing the sun up in the sky when it should be night. And I was blown away by the grand beauty of Vancouver. It was all so dramatic and postcard gorgeous."

Ayelet's daughter watching goats in Tel Aviv, Israel.
AYELET TSABARI

Ayelet grew up in a large family of Yemeni descent, and her grandparents were immigrants who settled in Israel in the 1930s. Her family was part of a minority whose culture was devalued and not represented in movies, music or television. "Growing up, I didn't see myself and my family represented in books—and I loved books—and in the media, which made me question my belonging," she tells me. "In Israel, like in many places, the dominant culture is European."

Israel was, and continues to be, immersed in conflict, and that had a huge impact on Ayelet's feelings of restlessness. "It's been in war since its inception, [and] while it wasn't always felt where I lived, that kind of threat and tension affected me as it affects everyone. It's ingrained in Israeli culture and experience. I was more on edge living there."

In addition to her social and political reasons for leaving, Ayelet had another, far more personal one. Her much-loved father died when she was just 10 years old. "Losing my father at a time when my identity was still very much entwined with his made me feel rootless and homeless, like I belonged nowhere," she reflects. By the time she was in her 20s, she was ready to come to Canada and begin again. "While I'd traveled extensively by that time, I'd never been that far away from home. It really felt like I was on the other side of the world. I loved that feeling. Like I could start again and be anyone I wanted to be."

Ayelet's daughter on one of their trips.
AYELET TSABARI

In Vancouver Ayelet slowly began to settle. "That first year was definitely the hardest. I remember looking from my downtown balcony at all the buildings and all the windows and the people inside of them and thinking there was not a single door I could knock on, and I was filled with intense loneliness," she tells me. Eventually, as she got to know people and the city, she felt more comfortable. "I built a life there. Made lifelong friends. And while I didn't stay with the man who made me move to Canada in the first place, I did end up meeting the love of my life there, and eventually we had a child together." Ayelet established her career as a writer in Vancouver, where there is a thriving literary community, and she is now an award-winning author of fiction and nonfiction.

Ayelet's partner and daughter on a hike.
AYELET TSABARI

In 2018 Ayelet, her partner and her six-year-old daughter decided to move again, this time back to Ayelet's hometown of Tel Aviv, where much of her family still lives. "I moved back because I wanted to be near my family and my mom, who's growing older and needs more help," she explains. "I also wanted my kid to have a relationship with her family, her grandmother and her cousins."

This move made the experience of migration far more real to Ayelet's daughter, who was born in Canada. When I ask what she misses most about Canada, she quickly answers, "My friends." At the same time, she loves Tel Aviv, especially, she says, "my new school and friends. And the beach."

In 2019 Ayelet published a book called *The Art of Leaving*, which is all about her journey from Tel Aviv and what prompted her to look for home in other places. Politics, love and grief may have made her explore the world, but it was family who brought her back. As she explains, "I missed the closeness of family more once I started my own."

DANNY RAMADAN

An International Activist

In 2019 Vancouver-based author Danny Ramadan received his Canadian citizenship. Danny's journey to Canada, during which he spent time in Egypt and Lebanon, was anything but simple. He explains, "I learned that I don't have to belong to one land and call it mine. I can belong to many lands and feel a sense of belonging and protection and carry all of these lands within my heart."

Danny was born in Syria to a large working-class family. In retrospect, he says, he thinks his father always knew that Danny was gay. "He set out to try and change that about me. He enrolled me in a religious school, aggressive sports, and got me a job as an electrician's apprentice." At age 17 Danny came out to his father and was immediately told to leave the family home. He lived on the streets for a while before finding work, eventually becoming a writer and journalist and writing his first book, a collection of short stories. His career led him to Cairo, Egypt, where he lived for several years.

In 2010, during the Arab Spring protests that changed much of the Middle East, Danny returned to Syria, hoping to learn more about his culture and community. "I was interested in learning more about our traditions, our stories and the way we understand the world around us. As well, I was interested in covering the political stories of Syria as the country headed toward what started as peaceful protests but ended up as civil war."

Back in his home country, Danny and a good friend started an underground LGBTQ+ center in Damascus that offered support to people grappling with gender and sexual identity. "We had a spare bedroom for folks kicked out of their homes, like what happened to me," he explains. "We held gatherings, some of them for fun and games, like cards and backgammon, and others so everyone could watch movies that were banned in Syria." This work, founded on kindness and empathy, is something Danny is very proud of.

Danny with his fiancé.
DANNY RAMADAN

Two years after starting the center, however, Danny was arrested for his activism, and he spent six weeks in prison. After his release he fled to Lebanon, where he started a second LGBTQ+ center, which was often used by fellow refugees. "My best memories of that house is the freedom we got as queer people to gather around, tell our stories, drink our tea as we shared tales of survival and resilience," he recalls. "It saddens me to hear the narrative of refugees being 'weaker than' or 'needy,' when in reality all the stories I heard were stories of strength and power of people not only challenged by the civil war but also challenged by the homophobic world they were born into. I think these people, my people, are peaceful warriors capable of so much beauty and so much creation."

In 2014 Danny arrived in Vancouver, British Columbia. He remembers those first few months as being idyllic. "I was taken aback by how relaxed, easygoing and clean Vancouver is," he tells me. "I remember my first Canada Day here, when I walked with my new friends to Stanley Park and found a small spot for a picnic. We sat together, my date in my lap, and I felt like the whole country was one big family

Danny speaking at an event honoring refugees and immigrants.
DANNY RAMADAN

celebrating one beautiful moment while watching fireworks. This resonated with me, coming from a land where families are the base of all your social interactions. I feel that I have a spiritual family here, which is a feeling I will never forget."

Settling in Canada came with its challenges too. At first Danny struggled with the differing ways Canadians and Syrians use language and conversation to connect with each other. "I arrived speaking English fluently, but that doesn't mean I didn't struggle with language. The first topic of discussion between Canadians is the weather. It's a social cue that they would like to start with small talk to get to know you. In Syria we rarely talk about the weather, and talking about it is a sign that the conversation is winding down. So many of my first attempts at integration here were lost in translation. While many Canadians were trying to get to know me, I got the impression that they were not interested."

The challenges were not limited to just conversation. Like many newcomers, Danny found it difficult to find a job, even with his background in writing and journalism. As well, he found himself "facing racist stereotypes about Arabs, Syrians and refugees."

In 2017 Danny published his critically acclaimed first novel, *The Clothesline Swing*. His children's book *Salma the Syrian Chef* was published in 2020. He enrolled in the Master of Fine Arts in Creative Writing program at the University of British Columbia in 2018 and got engaged to be married that same year. Applying for his Canadian citizenship seemed like a natural step.

"I remember the day of my oath ceremony—January 31, 2019—when I realized that I'd become Canadian. I realized that I belong to this nation now and carry with me the responsibilities that all of its citizens carry with them.

Responsibilities such as voting, volunteering and respecting the First Nations folks."

When I ask Danny what he thinks children should know about refugees, his answer is perfectly in tune with his journey to Canada, one that has been layered with his many different experiences, challenges and triumphs. "I think children should realize that each refugee has their own story. Each refugee is an individual with their own cultural background, nationality, religion, racial identity, sexual orientation and gender identity, among other things. It's important that we do not rely on stereotypes. There are so many beautiful stories to learn and cultures to visit and identities to explore within this community."

Conclusion

When I started writing this book, I had no idea how much I would learn. Migration is something that I, like many people, have taken for granted, as it is part of my family history and part of the histories of so many people I know. It was not a process I'd thought about, but rather one that I accepted as part of the human experience around me. After all, my extended family not only moved from China to Canada, but also to Cuba, Australia and the United States.

However, as I researched how people come to move and settle in places far away from their original homes, I learned that migration is a unique experience for each family and each person. Sometimes people are fleeing a war that has destroyed their homes. Sometimes people are looking for better jobs. Sometimes people have been persecuted and fear for their safety. And their journeys don't end with leaving their communities. In their new homes they learn languages, systems and cultures, find support with new friends and do their best to make a safe and happy home for their children and grandchildren.

Syrian refugee children in a classroom in Istanbul, Turkey.
TOLGA SEZGIN/SHUTTERSTOCK.COM

While each experience is different, some aspects of migration are universal. After all, for as long as humans have existed, they have searched for new homes. It's a basic human right to look for ways to build the life you want, whether that means applying to the right school or choosing your own friends or finding a city and a country where you can live freely and without fear. Refugees and immigrants, like all of us, are looking for a place to settle in which their families can grow and be happy. This journey, which can span the globe or cross a border, is one that touches us all.

ANDREY_POPOV/SHUTTERSTOCK.COM

GLOSSARY

asylum seekers—people who have fled their home country and are waiting to be evaluated and resettled by another country or organization that will offer them protection

child soldier—a child under the age of 18 who has been forced to join a militia or rebel group and participate in acts related to war or terrorism

colonization—when one group of people forces its way into another group's community and takes control of its government, population and resources

decolonization—when a government hands over control to one of its colonies, allowing that colony to achieve governmental and financial independence; the term can also refer to the long process of undoing some of the harm a government or system has caused to people who have historically been discriminated against and whose country was once colonized by another

emigration—the movement of people out of their communities

forcibly displaced people—people who, because of violence and war or religious and political persecution, are no longer safe in their homes and have to flee in order to keep themselves and their families safe

human migration—the movement of people away from their homes to establish new ones in other places; the term is often used in describing how humans established themselves around the world

human trafficking—moving people who are vulnerable to other countries, via criminal networks, and forcing them to work for little or no pay at jobs that break labor and human-rights laws, such as sex work

illegal migrants—people who cross a border and enter a country by violating the immigration rules of that country

immigrants—people who move permanently to a country they were not born in or haven't lived in previously

immigration—the movement of people into communities with the intention of settling as residents or citizens

indentured laborers—people who have been trafficked, or who have paid traffickers to help them reach a country of safety, and have been promised payment and/or freedom once they have worked for a certain amount of time to pay off their debt to the traffickers

internally displaced persons—people who are seeking safety within their own country

marginalization—when a group of people is denied its rights by a majority group with power, either through official policies or through social and cultural oppression

migrants—people who move from one country to another; the term is most often applied to people who are seeking asylum or trying to move to a country with better opportunities in education, work and healthcare

push and pull factors—reasons people decide to move permanently to a new country; a *pull* factor is something that attracts a person, such as better opportunities for work, schooling or personal goals, while a *push* factor is something that compels them to leave, such as war, persecution and lack of jobs

refugee camp—a community that develops when large numbers of asylum seekers flee to a specific location; it is governed by a refugee-aid organization, and refugee claims are often assessed there

refugees—people who are forced to move away from their homes because of war, persecution or crime

resettlement—the process of moving refugees to a different home and helping them learn its systems, language and culture

slavery—the practice of forcing people into unpaid labor, usually with poor living and working conditions, by a group of people who trade, buy and sell humans for this purpose

stateless persons—people who are not citizens of any country, which can be the result of rapid change in that country due to war or persecution

undocumented—a person who moves to another country and remains there without legal documentation; they could be an asylum seeker or a person looking to improve the quality of life for themselves and their families

United Nations Refugee Agency—an agency, also known as the Office of the United Nations High Commissioner for Refugees (UNHCR), that organizes and approves refugee claims worldwide and advocates for the rights of refugees, asylum seekers and other displaced persons

RESOURCES

Print

Kakuma Girls: Sharing Stories of Hardship and Hope from Kakuma Refugee Camp
by Clare Morneau and contributors
(Barlow Books)
This book features writing from 10 girls who attend the Morneau Shepell Secondary School for Girls at the Kakuma Refugee Camp in Kenya. Through letters, stories and photographs, these young women show what life in the world's largest refugee camp is really like.

Child Soldier: When Boys and Girls Are Used in War
by Michel Chikwanine and Jessica Dee Humphreys
(Kids Can Press)
A graphic novel by child soldier survivor and refugee Michel Chikwanine, this book tells his story, from the moment he was kidnapped from a school soccer game in the Democratic Republic of Congo to his years forced to fight with a rebel militia to his escape and resettlement in Canada.

I Am Malala: The Girl Who Stood Up for Education and Was Shot by the Taliban
by Malala Yousafzai with Christina Lamb
(Little, Brown and Company)
A memoir from the youngest recipient of the Nobel Peace Prize, Malala Yousafzai, this book is about her activism on behalf of girls in Pakistan, the attack meant to silence her and her recovery.

Duran Duran, Imelda Marcos and Me
by Lorina Mapa
(Conundrum Press)
This graphic memoir chronicles Lorina Mapa's childhood in the Philippines, her family's involvement in the 1986 People Power Revolution, and the music that comforted her through political instability, immigration to the United States and her father's death.

You Bring the Distant Near
by Mitali Perkins
(Farrar, Strauss and Giroux)
This award-winning young-adult novel weaves the stories of three generations of teens in one Indian American family. From a grandmother worried about the loss of their culture to a daughter who falls in love with an American boy to a granddaughter who returns to India as an activist, this novel explores all the ways immigrant identity can exist in one family.

Online

Children on the Run: Stories
Report produced by UNHCR
unhcr.org/news/stories/2016/4/56fe41a3125/children-on-the-run-stories.html
In their own words, over 400 children from Honduras, Guatemala and El Salvador share their stories of fleeing their homes and seeking safety.

Map of Human Migration
Interactive website produced by *National Geographic*
genographic.nationalgeographic.com/human-journey
Follow the paths of the earliest human migrants as they spread across the globe.

Stories and Features
Personal stories curated by UNICEF
unicef.org/stories
Read stories and view photographs of children and their families worldwide who face challenges because of conflict, lack of resources and political instability.

Canadian Museum of Immigration at Pier 21
Interactive website produced by the Canadian Museum of Immigration
pier21.ca/home
Explore the museum's virtual exhibitions about newcomers, their histories and their legacies.

Immigration Timeline
The history of American immigration, produced by The Statue of Liberty—Ellis Island Foundation
libertyellisfoundation.org/immigration-timeline
Learn about immigration to the United States from pre-1790 to the present day.

Video

Immigrants in Canada: Watch 5 Films That Explore Their Journey
From the National Film Board of Canada
blog.nfb.ca/blog/2018/10/10/immigrants-immigration-films
Watch five documentaries from the NFB archives that explore all the ways immigrants live, work and love in Canada.

Which Way Home
Directed by Rebecca Cammisa
whichwayhome.net
This Academy Award–nominated documentary follows the lives of unaccompanied children who are traveling to the United States, hoping for better lives.

Inocente
Directed by Sean Fine and Andrea Nix Fine
inocentedoc.com
Winner of the Academy Award for Best Documentary (Short Subject), this film follows 15-year-old Inocente, an undocumented immigrant living in San Diego, California, who dreams of becoming a famous artist.

Underwater Dreams
Directed by Mary Mazzio
underwaterdreamsfilm.com
This feature documentary spotlights a team of high-school students from Phoenix, Arizona, all of whom are children of undocumented Mexican immigrants, who invented a prize-winning underwater robot that went on to defeat a team from MIT.

ACKNOWLEDGMENTS

To Sarah Harvey, who challenged me to write the inclusive book I had always dreamed of.

To the team at Orca Books—Andrew Wooldridge, Ruth Linka, Jen Cameron and everyone else—for giving me the opportunity to reach the best readers in the world.

To Drew Shannon, for the beautifully human illustrations in his book.

To the lovely humans who allowed me to interview them for this book—Baharak Yousefi, Gaby, Juan and Maya Gomez, Daniel Saiyo, Mishal Saeed, Asia Capri, Reem Shehadat and Ibrahim, Mohammad and Khaleel Jaridi, Nhung N. Tran-Davies, Ruquya Al-itbi, Mariana Veiga, Samer Muscati, Omar Akubar, Ayelet Tsabari and Danny Ramadan—your lives and words illuminate this book and have continued to inspire me to do better and work harder.

To my writerly friends—Dina Del Bucchia, Andrea MacPherson, June Hutton, Mary Novik, Shawn Krause, Stacey May Fowles, Carleigh Baker, Chelsea Rooney, Amber Dawn, Robin Stevenson, Paul Vermeersch, David Ly and Ben Rawluk—for listening to me talk about this book, for offering suggestions, for feeding me or transporting me when the need arose, all the love.

To Carolyn Swayze, for keeping me organized and always believing I can write it all.

To Jeff, for loving and listening, and also for reminding me that politics are bigger than we are, but that none of us is too small to make change.

And, finally, to Oscar and Rosie, my little family, the loves of my life.

INDEX

*Page numbers in **bold** indicate an image caption.*

Jen Sookfong Lee was born and raised on Vancouver's East Side, and she now lives with her son in North Burnaby. Her books include *The Conjoined*, nominated for the International Dublin Literary Award and a finalist for the Ethel Wilson Fiction Prize; *The Better Mother*, a finalist for the City of Vancouver Book Award; *The End of East*; *Gentlemen of the Shade* and *The Animals of Chinese New Year*. Jen teaches at The Writer's Studio Online with Simon Fraser University, edits fiction for Wolsak & Wynn and co-hosts the literary podcast *Can't Lit*.